A PRACTICAL GUIDE FOR FACILITATING BEHAVIORAL/ PSYCHIATRIC ASSESSMENT FOR PERSONS WITH MENTAL RETARDATION

By
Ann R. Poindexter, M.D.

2002
The NADD Press, Kingston, NY

An association for persons with developmental disabilities and mental health needs.

132 Fair Street
Kingston, New York 12401

Library of Congress Number: 2002113069

ISBN 1-57256-035-5

1st Printing 2002

Printed in the United States of America

TABLE OF CONTENTS

FOREWORD

One of the most important and exciting current areas of interest for both professionals and nonprofessionals involved in providing services for persons with developmental disabilities, as well as for people working in the mental health care field, is "dual diagnosis"—diagnosis and treatment of behavioral/psychiatric problems in persons with mental retardation and other developmental disabilities. (Many people who work in mental health also use the term "dual diagnosis" to indicate the presence of both of a substance abuse disorder and another mental health disorder.)

In the past many of us were taught that people with developmental disabilities were not smart enough to have "real" psychiatric problems. In contrast, we may have been told that severely withdrawn persons with mental retardation obviously had psychiatric problems because they were severely withdrawn, or that aggressive persons with mental retardation obviously had psychiatric problems because they were aggressive. Some "experts" even told us that persons with mental retardation could not have personality disorders because they didn't have personalities(!). We may even have been taught that all kinds of behavior in these persons should be treated with medications, particularly neuroleptics ("major" tranquilizers), and if we could just make them more quiet, we could say we had helped them.

Estimates of the prevalence of psychiatric disorders in people with mental retardation in community and clinical populations range from 14.3 to 67.3 percent (Campbell & Malone, 1991). A wide range of psychiatric conditions have been reported in people with mental retardation, and the prevalence of specific disorders varies from report to report. Rates are infuenced by methodology, study setting, sample selection, level of mental retardation and age, and the diagnostic criteria used. At least some of the difference in prevalence rates probably reflects particular demographic differences in the groups studied (Poindexter, Bihm, & Litton, 1996). Rates of psychiatric disorders among people with mental retardation can be overestimated by the inclusion of non-specific behavioral disturbances that may on occasion be explainable by retardation, such as wandering and stealing (Vitiello & Behar, 1992). While the deinstitutionalization and normalization movements have led to integration of many people with mental retardation into the community, the significance (and often the seriousness) of the presence of behavioral/psychiatric problems in these individuals may not have been fully recognized. This lack of appreciation of problems may be an example of a wider tendency to deny or minimize serious mental illness in general, a case of ideology winning out over clinical reality (Lamb, 1997).

Trends in health care for persons with mental retardation have often involved systematic tapering of neuroleptic drugs, earlier by court mandate, administrative order, or voluntarily, and more recently because of interpretation of federal regulations. These tapers have revealed the frequent occurrence of nondyskinetic and/or dyskinetic drug withdrawal syndromes. Additionally, a significant number of persons have developed obvious emergent psychiatric symptoms as well, which had apparently been more or less masked by the long-term neuroleptic medications previously prescribed. In apparent contrast to earlier approaches, more recent federal surveyor guidelines have noted the importance of careful assessment for possible psychiatric diagnosis, and provision of rational drug treatments if appropriate for the diagnosis (Health Care Financing Administration, 1996). Also, emphasis on an interdisciplinary approach for provision of services has put in place an important information-gathering source for facilitation of diagnosis of psychiatric disorders in general.

This volume is designed to assist members of interdisciplinary teams and others in collecting and providing information to facilitate accurate psychiatric diagnosis for individuals with complex mental health/behavioral problems. This is not intended merely as an intellectual exercise, but as a practical means of understanding an individual and his/her problems, and as an aid for development of a rational treatment program, either behavioral, pharmacologic, ecologic, psychotherapeutic, or any combination of the four. The appendix of this volume includes five self-directed instructional programs for staff members and others, dealing with an overview of dual diagnosis, depression, anxiety disorders, psychosis, and personality disorders. (The program on anxiety disorders has been previously published by NADD Press in a monograph on anxiety disorders.)

—Ann R. Poindexter, M.D.

CHAPTER ONE

DEVELOPING AN INFORMATION MANAGEMENT SYSTEM FOR "DUAL-DIAGNOSIS"

Obviously no single model will be appropriate for every situation in which individuals need evaluation for psychiatric/behavioral disorders. In most settings a suitable format will have to evolve, through trial and error, as members of the interdisciplinary team or other group search for strategies to help persons with complex behavior problems. While no one expects to make psychiatrists out of interdisciplinary team members, one study that examined the test-retest reliability of team consensus best-estimate diagnoses of Axis I and II psychiatric disorders as reflected in *Diagnostic and statistical manual of mental disorders, 4th edition (DSM-IV)* (American Psychiatric Association, 1994) found this process to have good to excellent reliability (Klein, Ouimette, Kelly, Ferro, & Riso, 1994), at least in a sample with the general population.

The first decision to be made is who will make the final diagnosis. Many experienced professionals in the field of developmental disabilities feel that "all psychiatrists are not created equal," at least as far as working with persons with mental retardation. Some psychiatrists are not particularly interested in working with this population, and these wishes should be honored as much as possible (Torrey, 1993). Some non-psychiatrist physicians and some psychologists are comfortable in making these diagnostic decisions, and some are not. Whoever is selected to consult for a definitive diagnosis should be well-versed in the sometimes atypical manifestations of psychiatric illness in persons with developmental disabilities.

Precision of diagnosis is greatly strengthened by the furnishing of appropriate information to the diagnosing clinician, particularly since many individuals with developmental disabilities have limited verbal skills. Caregivers are a very valuable source of clinical data, but by nature these are secondary sources. Because the caretaker is not a primary source, information may be somewhat biased for one reason or another (Hurley & Sovner, 1992). Also, the information given may be incomplete because observations are based on limited contact with the person. An additional problem may develop if the caregivers have not been trained to recognize signs of psychopathology (Holt, 1998). Despite the communication difficulties that are often present, the affected person should be interviewed, as well as caregivers, if at all possible, since studies show considerable disagreement between interviews with the person themselves and with informants (Moss, Prosser, Ibbotson, & Goldberg, 1996).

This author has had extensive experience with two functional models for data collection in an institutional setting, which may also have relevance for persons who live in other, less restrictive, settings. (Unfortunately, to my knowledge neither of these models is presently in use, not because they were considered ineffective, but at least partially because other suitable forms of psychiatric consultation became more readily available.) One model, developed at Conway Human Development Center in Conway, Arkansas, involved referral to a dual diagnosis committee from the individual's interdisciplinary team, either from annual staffing or special staffing. Time of evaluation was scheduled by the committee co-chair, the facility chief psychologist. The committee then met to review background information and interview and/or observe the individual. Standing committee members included all facility physicians, including the medical director, and all facility PhD-level psychologists, including the chief psychologist. Medical director and chief psychologist were co-chairpersons. Attendance at committee meetings included standing members, the individual himself/herself, direct support personnel, QMRP, family members, the individual's psychologic examiner, and any others who could provide relevant information. The medical history was reviewed by the individual's primary physician. Behavioral history was reviewed by the psychologic examiner, and included past behavioral history and treatments and current behaviors and treatment programs. The individual was interviewed if appropriate, and direct care personnel were interviewed extensively. Other data were presented if relevant. *Diagnostic and Statistical Manual of Mental Disorders (Third Edition, Revised) (DSM-III-R)* criteria for diagnoses were reviewed, and diagnosis was made by consensus of committee members. Summaries of proceedings and diagnostic decisions were filed in Central Records, and information added to computer data base file to facilitate systematic updating and review.

In another model, that developed at Developmental Center in Grafton, North Dakota, members of the medical staff and psychology staff met on a regular monthly basis as a diagnostic review committee to review diagnostic issues for each resident of the facility, just prior to his/her annual team review. Attendance included physicians, nurse practitioners/physician assistants, and PhD and masters-level psychologists. Appropriate additional testing and evaluation was outlined, and was performed by assigned professionals before the next meeting. Diagnoses were made by consensus of committee members, utilizing DSM-III-R criteria, and were added to the computer data base file. Referrals were also made to this committee from team reviews at times other than the annual review, if the team felt this was necessary.

CHAPTER TWO

THE MENTAL HEALTH CONSULTATION

After a decision has been made to refer an individual for a mental health consultation, as much information as possible should be collected and provided to the consultant. Sovner and Hurley (1983a) have provided a list of types of information which should be collected. This list includes the reason for the referral, the length of time the problem has been present, and what makes the problem better or worse. Other additional information about the problem is a listing of any significant emotional or physical events which occurred immediately before the problem began. Information related to the individual's cognitive (thought) level, most recent psychological test results, and the cause(s) of the mental retardation (if known) should be listed. The person's psychosocial status, including his/her current living and social arrangements, educational, vocational, and recreational programs, should be outlined, and name of primary contact persons should be clearly presented.

Other very important information to be provided includes current medical problems, with a list of diagnoses, the treatment that is in place, and where the treatment is occurring. For each prescribed drug, the name, dosage, administration schedule, and prescribing physician should be listed. Nonprescription drugs and herbal/nutritional preparations should also be listed.

Any previous mental health interventions, including dates of treatment, type of problem, and name of treating clinician or mental health agency, should be listed. Any family history of mental illness, including the type problem, treatment dates, and name of the treating clinician or mental health agency, should be provided.

Any changes in vegetative functioning and behavior should be carefully sought out and described, including energy level, appetite, weight change, and sleep pattern. Urinary and/or fecal incontinence should be described if this is new behavior.

Carefully edited videotapes of any sort of behavior which may appear strange and/or difficult to describe may be of help if provided to a mental health consultant. When the individual is seen in the consultant's office, a person who knows him/her well should accompany the individual, to provide any additional information which the consultant may need. Most professionals who work with people with mental retardation and behavioral/psychiatric problems perform a mental status examination as a part of their clinical assessment, either formally or informally. (Many others who work closely with these individuals do the same thing, often unconsciously.) Sovner and Hurley (1983b) discuss factors usually assessed in a mental status examination, and note the importance of factoring in the severity of the individual's developmental disability, since marked impairment may decrease the areas and levels of functioning that can be assessed.

A mental status examination begins the instant the interview with the person begins (Cummings, 1993). From that moment on, the examiner gathers information about the person's language skills, knowledge of his/her medical history, and ability to maintain attention and concentration. This early knowledge lets the examiner make decisions about the type questions most appropriate for the person. In assessment of an individual's general behavior and appearance, areas noted are level of activity and purposefulness, amount of contact with the environment, facial expressions, and any unusual behaviors and/or postures (Sovner & Hurley, 1983b). Speech and thought processes are assessed by attempting to note the degree of speech productivity, which includes whether or not they speak spontaneously and whether or not their speech imitates others or is perseverative (repeating the same words over and over). The rate of speaking, degree of organization of speech, and content of speech are noted.

Apparent mood and affect are assessed by looking for a range of expression of emotions—does the person appear exuberant, withdrawn, or "flat?" Attention is paid to whether or not expressions of emotion are appropriate to the content of speech and/or outside events, as well as whether the mood seems to be "up and down." Any pervasive mood such as sadness, anger, euphoria ("a high"), or irritability is described.

Another area of assessment includes the presence or absence of any symptoms of psychosis, such as hallucinations and/or delusions. Hallucinations are experienced as hearing, seeing, smelling, tasting, or touching something which is not there. Delusions are incorrect beliefs that usually involve a misinterpretation of perceptions or experiences. If other psychiatric conditions such as phobias (fears), apparent compulsions, and/or obsessions are present, these facts are noted.

Some assessment of cognitive (thought) function is made in a mental status examination, including the individual's orientation as to who and where he/she is, the day, and perhaps the date. Attention, concentration, and memory are evaluated, and note is made of social and academic achievement.

In 1986 Sovner and Hurley described four non-specific factors associated with mental retardation which influence the process of making a psychiatric diagnosis. The first factor, intellectual distortion, is defined as the effect(s) of concrete thinking and impaired communication skills, often resulting in inability of the individual to label and report his/her own experiences. The second described factor is psychosocial, defined as effects of impoverished social skills and life experiences. These often result clinically in unsophisticated presentation and lack of poise during an interview, which may lead either to missed symptoms or misdiagnosis of nervousness and "silliness" as psychiatric symptoms.

A third factor which may influence the process of making a psychiatric diagnosis is cognitive disintegration, defined as the effects of disturbance of information processing caused by stress. These effects may cause the individual to look peculiar, even psychotic, perhaps leading to a misdiagnosis of schizophrenia. Sovner and Hurley's fourth factor is baseline exaggeration, defined as increase in severity of pre-existing cognitive (thought) deficits and maladaptive behaviors, due to a psychiatric disorder. This factor causes problems in establishing the features of the psychiatric disorder, target symptoms, and outcome measures.

CHAPTER THREE

USING THE DSM-IV

The American Psychiatric Association published a fourth edition of its *Diagnostic and Statistical Manual of Mental Disorders*, better known as DSM-IV, in 1994, to assist with classification of mental disorders. A text-revision was published in 2000. The DSM-IV clearly states an intent to think about each of a series of mental disorders as a clinically significant behavioral or psychological syndrome or pattern, occurring in a particular person, which is associated with present distress or disability, or with a significantly increased risk of suffering death, pain, disability, or an important loss of freedom. Additionally, the pattern must not be merely a culturally anticipated response to a particular event such as the death of a loved one. Particular mention is made that neither deviant behavior, in political, religious, or sexual areas for example, nor conflicts primarily occurring between the person and society at large are mental disorders unless the deviance or conflict is a symptom of a dysfunction in the person himself/herself.

DSM-IV does not classify people, but disorders that people have. Accordingly, the text itself is rather "person first," using terms such as "a person with schizophrenia" rather than "a schizophrenic."

No assumption is made in DSM-IV that each category of mental disorder is completely separate, with absolute borders dividing it from other mental disorders or from absence of a mental disorder. There also is no presumption that everyone described as having the same mental disorder is like everyone else with that disorder. Anyone using DSM-IV should remember that people sharing a diagnosis may be quite different in many ways, even in respect to the defining features of the diagnosis, and that many individuals may be difficult to diagnose in any way except according to the most probable diagnostic hypothesis ("best guess").

DSM-IV has a multiaxial (multiple part) system for evaluation, to make sure that certain information of value in planning treatment and predicting outcome for each person is recorded. This multiaxial system involves an assessment on five axes, each of which refers to a different area of information. Axis I is used for reporting all mental disorders in the classification except for personality disorders and mental retardation. In addition to clinical disorders, Axis I includes other conditions that might be a focus of clinical attention. A number of major groups make up Axis I disorders, including disorders usually first diagnosed in infancy, childhood, or adolescence, with the exception of mental retardation. (Other developmental disabilities such as autism are included in Axis I.) Other major groups of Axis I disorders are delirium, dementia, and amnestic and other cognitive disorders; mental disorders due to a general medical condition; substance-related disorders; schizophrenia and other psychotic disorders; mood disorders; anxiety disorders; somatoform disorders; factitious (artificial, created deliberately by the individual) disorders; dissociative disorders; sexual and gender identity disorders; eating disorders; sleep disorders; impulse-control disorders; adjustment disorders; and, as noted earlier, other conditions that may be a focus of clinical attention.

Axis II is used for reporting personality disorders and mental retardation.

Axis III is for reporting current general medical conditions that are possibly relevant to understanding or management of the person's mental disorder. Axis IV is used for reporting psychosocial and environmental problems, such as recent stressors, that may affect the diagnosis, treatment, and projected outcome of mental disorders.

Axis V is for reporting the judgment of the assessing clinician as to the person's overall level of functioning, utilizing the Global Assessment of Functioning (GAF) Scale, outlined on page 32 of DSM-IV, and further amplified in the DSM-IV appendix. While this scale appears to be difficult to use for people with significant developmental disabilities, at least by those inexperienced in working with this population, members of interdisciplinary teams may find it helpful in attempting to quantify both baseline levels and results of treatment programs. A similar scale has been found to be useful for inpatient psychiatric planning and evaluation for a group of state hospital admissions (Kuhlman, Sincaban, & Bernstein, 1990).

A version of DSM-IV designed for use by primary care providers was published by American Psychiatric Association in 1995. This version includes algorithms for common primary care presentations of mental health disorders, as well as a variety of helpful charts and other explanatory material. American Academy of Pediatrics published a child and adolescent version of DSM-IV for primary care providers in 1996, which also contains additional helpful materials. Two physicians (Frances & First, 1998) who were actively involved in the development of DSM-IV have recently published a guide to that volume for non-medical persons which appears to present a great deal of important information in a simplified, very practical format. (Persons of all clinical backgrounds with responsibility for program development and monitoring for people with mental retardation and significant behavioral/psychiatric problems will probably find this book very helpful.)

CHAPTER FOUR

HOLISTIC ASSESSMENT OF PSYCHOPATHOLOGY IN PERSONS WITH MENTAL RETARDATION

In an oral presentation at a national meeting of the National Association for the Dually Diagnosed (Mental Health and Mental Retardation) (1990), Robert Sovner listed five causes of psychopathology in persons with mental retardation: a) learned maladaptive behavior, b) central nervous system dysfunction, c) childhood onset pervasive developmental disorder, d) classic psychiatric disorder, and e) medical/drug-induced disorder. This type of differential diagnostic list can be quite useful as clinicians and other interdisciplinary team members attempt to to develop rational treatment programs by sorting out possible causes of difficult behavior problems. Each of these five causes fits into the DSM-IV classification scheme, and diagnoses/causes are not mutually exclusive. Often persons with developmental disabilities and behavior problems exhibit more than one of these causes. Pharmacologic intervention is not necessarily required for conditions in any of the five categories, but may be helpful in some circumstances.

(In the sections that follow, as an attempt to assist members of interdisciplinary teams and others trying to develop rational treatment programs for persons with complex behavioral patterns, discussion of each of the five categories is preceded by a brief section of questions to be asked and answered, as well as important clues to possible diagnostic postulates. Some sections also include related mnemonics.)

a) LEARNED MALADAPTIVE BEHAVIORS

Questions to ask:

- What purpose does this behavior serve?
- What makes this behavior worse?
- What makes this behavior better?

Important clues:

- The behavior often occurs when the individual is asked to do something they don't want to do.
- The behavior is very successful in enabling the individual to avoid something they don't want to do, or get something they want, such as attention.
- The behavior is not only successful, but is of long duration.
- The person has spent long periods of his/her life in places where the behavior was reinforced for one reason or another.

*****

Many persons with developmental disabilities have lived in settings for long periods of time where they have observed and often copied all kinds of maladaptive behaviors, or where various maladaptive behaviors have been reinforced for one reason or another. As an example, ear banging behavior may have originally started because of an earache, but then may have been found to be an effective way to avoid situations perceived as undesirable. As an example, if an individual bangs his ears he may not be required to take a bath. In the DSM-IV multiaxial system, this sort of behavior may be most appropriately coded as a "V Code," a condition not attributable to a mental disorder that is a focus of attention or treatment. Learned maladaptive behaviors exhibited by persons with developmental disabilities should probably be coded as V62.89, Phase of Life Problem (page 685), with further information included to indicate the nature of the life circumstance. If maladaptive behaviors appear to be due to prolonged institutionalization, that should be carefully noted.

When attempting to decide whether or not a particular behavior is at least to some degree "learned," most examiners perform some sort of functional analysis of the behavior (Gable, 1996). This term is sometimes used to refer to a specific clinical technique, in which the reinforcers of the behavior(s) are determined through systematic manipulation of the environment. Others apply the term functional analysis to the entire field of behavior analysis, which looks at behavior as a function of the environment. In this view, if something is known about the environment, behavior might be predicted, and if one is given enough control over the environment, behavior can be controlled (Bihm et al., 1996).

A recent survey noted that most professionals use functional assessment procedures in an attempt to identify what may be causing problems and/or influencing behavior patterns in persons with mental retardation (Desrochers, Hile, & Williams-Moseley, 1997). This survey found that indirect and descriptive assessments seem to be more useful than experimental manipulation. Indirect assessments refer to information-gathering procedures such as rating scales, interviews, role playing, and self-report. Descriptive observations refer to methods for observing and keeping record of behavior to identify the variables that affect the behavior (Desrochers et al., 1997).

In general, learned maladaptive behaviors are not particularly responsive to medication treatment. Successful treatment programs often require a combination of behavioral therapy and ecologic/environmental management, but these programs should never be considered particularly easy or simple, largely due to problems with using prescribed interventions in typical life settings, and the inability of some care providers to satisfactorily implement interventions (Lowry, 1993; Pyles, Muniz, Cade, & Silva, 1997). Successful behavioral treatment of a problem behavior may involve a number of interventions, each of which is directly related to the function of a behavior under a given circumstance. Treatment strategies which are minimally intrusive, and focus on teaching and encouraging adaptive skills, certainly can be effective (Lowry, 1993).

b) CENTRAL NERVOUS SYSTEM DYSFUNCTION

Questions to ask:

- Is this individual irritable, impulsive, short-tempered?
- Does this person appear to have a "short fuse?"
- Does this person have a history of hydrocephalus?

Important clues:

- The problem behavior occurs after very little provocation.
- The person has a history of brain damage.
- The person has epilepsy and/or cerebral palsy. (Certainly not everyone with these conditions has problem behavior!)
- The person has a history of hydrocephalus, and verbal ability far surpasses other functional abilities.

*****

Experts have known for a number of years that demonstrable neurologic defects are much more common in people with behavioral problems than in the general population. Episodic dyscontrol syndrome is defined by neurologists as a condition characterized by recurrent attacks of uncontrollable rage, usually with very little provocation, and often completely out of character (Elliot, 1984). Description of this syndrome seems very similar to several disorders described in DSM-IV, particularly intermittent explosive disorder (pages 609-612) and personality change due to a general medical condition (pages 171-174). Persons with intermittent explosive disorder have a history of several distinct episodes of loss of control of aggressive impulses, resulting in significant assaultive acts and/or destruction of property. The degree of expressed aggressiveness expressed during the episodes is far out of proportion to any precipitating stressors. For this specific diagnosis to be made, the episodes should not better be accounted for by some other mental disorder or effect of a substance such as a drug of abuse or a medication. In personality change due to a general medical condition (formerly called "organic personality disorder"), a persistent personality disturbance develops which represents a change from the person's previous pattern, and there is objective evidence that the disturbance is the direct result of a general medical condition. Several types are described, including labile, disinhibited, aggressive, apathetic, and paranoid.

One particular type of personality change due to general medical condition is referred to as "cocktail party" syndrome. This syndrome is seen relatively frequently in persons with the childhood form of hydrocephalus (Sovner & Hurley, 1982). These individuals have chatty speech, with superficial content and frequent use of short, stereotyped phrases. Verbal fluency is far superior to verbal content. People with cocktail party syndrome often appear to be emotionally labile, with poor judgement. They often seem maladjusted. Their I.Q. frequently is within the range for mental retardation, and there is a significant difference between verbal I.Q. and performance I.Q.. These individuals usually have poor academic, social, and vocational achievement.

Sovner and Hurley (1982a) stress the importance for families and staff treating people with cocktail party syndrome to have a realistic sense of the individual's abilities. They note that it is common for staff and family to expect far more than the person can produce in terms of vocational and academic goals. This seems to be particularly important during adolescence, as the affected individual attempts to assume the adult role. Pressure from others may cause him/her to blame self for failing to live up to expectations, and anxiety and depressive symptoms may develop.

c) PERVASIVE DEVELOPMENTAL DISORDERS

Questions to ask:

- Does this person have autism, Rett syndrome, or other diagnosed pervasive developmental disorder?
- Does this person's pervasive developmental disorder have any connection with his/her behavioral problems?
- If not formally diagnosed, does this person have major symptoms which are compatible with the diagnosis?

Important clues:

- The individual prefers very strict, consistent routines.
- The individual has qualitative problems with social interaction and communication.
- The person has many ritualistic behaviors.

Mnemonic for autistic disorder:

With routines and rituals has great comfort—

Has almost no ability to carry on a conversation—

All kinds of delays in spontaneous and creative play—

Takes great interest in strange things—

All kinds of stereotyped motor mannerisms—

Language development delayed—

Only wants to stay by himself/herself—

Non-verbal communication impaired—

Emotional and social reciprocity just not there—

Repetitive language mannerisms—

*****

DSM-IV (pages 66-71) notes that features essential for a diagnosis of autistic disorder are the presence of markedly abnormal or impaired development in social interaction and communication, and a very restricted group of activities and interests. Other common names for autistic disorder are early infantile autism, childhood autism, and Kanner's autism. The clinical picture of autistic disorder varies greatly, depending on the developmental level and chronological age of the individual, but all people with autism have a markedly restricted set of activities and interests.

About 75% of children with autistic disorder have some degree of mental retardation. Autistic disorder may be associated with abnormal findings on physical examination, or with general medical conditions such as phenylketonuria, tuberous sclerosis, fragile X syndrome, and maternal rubella syndrome, but many people with autism have completely normal physical examinations. About one-fourth of persons with autistic disorder also have a history of epilepsy (American Psychiatric Association, 1994a).

Males are four or five times as apt to have autistic disorder as are females, but females are more likely to have more associated severe mental retardation. Autistic disorder formerly was thought to occur in two to five persons per 10,000 individuals (American Psychiatric Association, 1994a), but some more recent data indicate a more common presence. Language skills and overall intellectual level appear to be the strongest factors related to ultimate prognosis (American Psychiatric Association, 1994a).

Qualitative impairment in social interaction may involve markedly atypical nonverbal behaviors, such as eye contact, facial expression, body postures, and gestures to regulate social interaction, as well as a failure to develop appropriate peer relationships. People with autism seldom choose to share enjoyment, interests, or achievements with others, and usually seem not to understand ordinary "give and take" of social relationships.

Qualitative impairments in communication may show up, in some cases, as marked delay in, or total lack of, development of spoken language, not accompanied by attempts at compensation through alternative ways of communication such as gestures or mime. In persons with adequate speech, marked impairment often exists in the ability to start or sustain a conversation with others, as well as frequent use of stereotyped, repetitive, and/or idiosyncratic language. People with autism who can speak are usually considered rather poor conversationalists.

Individuals with autistic disorder usually are not able to have spontaneous make-believe play, as appropriate for their level of development. They often are quite preoccupied with one or more stereotyped and restricted patterns of interest that may appear abnormal, either in intensity or focus. They often compulsively adhere to specific, non-functional routines or rituals, and/or have stereotyped and repetitive motor mannerisms such as finger flapping or twisting. They are often persistently preoccupied with parts of objects. (While many people have fixed daily routines and behaviors, people with autism often have very intense participation in these activities.)

Delays or abnormal functioning in social interaction, language as used for social communication, and/or symbolic or imaginative play begin before the age of three years. These delays may be somewhat subtle.

Rett disorder (DSM-IV pages 71-73), another pervasive developmental disorder, is typically associated with severe or profound mental retardation, and has only been reported in females. People with Rett disorder have increased frequency of EEG abnormalities and associated seizure disorders. Rett disorder is much more rare than autistic disorder. Girls with Rett disorder appear normal very early in life, with a normal head circumference at birth. Head growth slows down between ages five and 48 months, and there is loss of previously acquired purposeful hand skills between ages five and 30 months. Stereotyped hand movements, which appear to be "hand-wringing" or "hand-washing," develop later. Persons with Rett syndrome develop a poorly coordinated gait, and may eventually stop walking. They have severely impaired expressive and receptive language development and severe psychomotor retardation.

Another pervasive developmental disorder, childhood disintegrative disorder, is also known as Heller syndrome, dementia infantilis, and disintegrative psychosis (DSM-IV pages 73-75). This condition is felt to be very rare, occurring much less frequently than autistic disorder. It probably occurs more commonly in males, and usually is associated with severe mental retardation. People with Heller syndrome appear normal for at least the first two years of life, and then lose previously acquired skills before the age of ten. This disorder usually develops between three and four years of age. Affected persons lose skills in language, social areas, bowel and bladder control, play, and motor areas. Symptoms of disintegrative disorder of childhood are similar to symptoms of autistic disorder, except for age of onset. An interesting recent study (Lewine et al., 1999) of children with austism spectrum disorders who had normal early development followed by an autistic regression between the ages of two and three utilized magnetoencephalography, a noninvasive method for identifying zones of abnormal brain activity, to study patterns of seizure activity during stage III sleep. Researchers found that a subset of children with these disorders demonstrated clinically relevant epileptiform activity during slow-wave sleep, even occasionally in the absence of a clinical seizure activity. They felt that if this epileptic activity is present, treatment strategies amined at its control might lead to improvement in language and autistic features. This remains, of course, to be proven, a fact that was pointed out by Neville (1999) in a commentary in the same publication as the original article.

Another pervasive developmental disorder, Asperger disorder, is not, by definition, associated with delays in language or any clinically significant delay in cognitive development (American Psychiatric Association, 1994a, pages 75-77). Affected individuals have severe and sustained impairment in social interaction, and develop restricted, repetitive patterns of behavior. Persons with Asperger disorder have significant impairment in social, occupational, and/or other important areas of functioning. Prevalence rates are unknown, but Asperger disorder is probably more common in males. It is usually first noticed somewhat later than is autistic disorder, and there seems to be some familial increase in incidence. Motor milestones may be somewhat delayed, and persons with this condition often appear clumsy.

d) CLASSIC PSYCHIATRIC DISORDER(S)

(Note: Questions to ask, important clues, and related mnemonics are listed prior to discussion of each disorder.)

Reported estimates of incidence of mental health disorders in persons with mental retardation vary from twenty to sixty percent (Fletcher & Poindexter, 1996; Poindexter et al., 1996), as compared to roughly 30% of Americans who reported a psychiatric disorder in the preceding year, according to a study in which a large national sample of people were interviewed (Miller, 1994). While many experienced clinicians state that psychiatric disorders occur more often in people with mental retardation that in a nonretarded population (Menolascino & Fleisher, 1993), Reiss pointed out in 1994 that at that time no research studies had been reported which directly compared the rates of mental disorders in people with mental retardation to the population as a whole. Persons with mental retardation certainly may have any mental health problem that anyone else has, but diagnosis may be more difficult in this group, due to problems with communication, and other factors previously mentioned (Sovner, 1996).

Depression

Questions to ask:

- Does this person seem "not like himself/herself?"
- Has this person's weight changed (either up or down) significantly

lately?

- Have this person's sleep habits changed?
- Does this person seem quieter than usual, and not as interested in usually preferred activities?
- Have this person's I.Q. or adaptive behavior level decreased appreciably lately?
- Have his/her job productivity or school performance decreased lately?
- Does this person seem sad and cry a lot?

Important clues:

- Any "yes" to any of the above questions.

Mnemonic for Major Depressive Episode:

Significant weight change, either up or down—

Observable psychomotor retardation or agitation—

Very low, depressed mood most of the time—

Extreme loss of interest or pleasure in most everything—

Real feelings of fatigue and loss of energy—

Yet more feelings of worthlessness and guilt—

Sleep either not enough or too much—

Ability to think and/or concentrate diminished—

Death on the mind—

*****

Depression is a very common type of mental illness, affecting millions of people in the United States every year. In a study of prevalence of depressive symptoms in primary care medical practice, Zung and group (1993) obtained survey data from a sample of over 75,000 patients who visited the offices of 765 primary care physicians for any reason from February to September, 1991. The outcome measurement used was the index score for the presence of depressive symptoms on the Zung Self-rating Depression Scale. The overall prevalence of significant symptoms of depression was 20.9%, but only 1.2% cited depression as the reason for their medical visit. In a somewhat similar study by Rowe and group (1995), 1898 patients were studied, from 88 primary care practices, using a self-administered health-habits questionnaire. Depression was assessed for both lifetime and for the past 30 days, using *Diagnostic and Statistical Manual of Mental Disorders, Third Edition Revised* (DSM-III-R) criteria. Of this group, a total of 21.7% of women and 12.7% of men met DSM-III-R criteria for depression in the 30 days prior to completing the survey. Lifetime rates of depression were 36.1% for women and 23.3% for men.

Up to one in eight individuals may require treatment for depression during their lifetime. Women are two to three times more apt to develop depression than are men, across all age groups. Point prevalence for major depressive disorder in western industrialized nations is 2.3 to 3.2 percent for men and 4.5 to 9.3 percent for women. Lifetime risk is 7 to 12 percent for men and 20 to 25 percent for women (Agency for Health Care Policy and Research, 1993).

Several large recent studies suggest that the incidence of depression is increasing, particularly in persons born since World War II. The age of onset seems to be decreasing, with new cases often developing in late teenage and early adult years (Klerman & Weissman, 1989; Cross-National Collaborative Group, 1992).

While the cause of depression is unknown, it seems to be the result of interaction between many factors. Most clinicians support a risk factor model that reflects varying contributions of biological (including genetic), psychological, and environmental factors. Depression tends to "run in families," which indicates a genetic influence, especially in severe cases. Depression seems to be more common in people from lower socioeconomic groups and in unmarried men (Council on Scientific Affairs, 1993).

Depression often develops following severely stressful life events, so that both circumstances and heredity seem to be frequently involved at the beginning of an episode of depression (Council on Scientific Affairs, 1993). Frequency of depressive disorders increases in people with medical illness, particularly cardiovascular disease, cancer, and neurologic disorders (Ferris, 1995).

Depressive disorders are frequently serious, life-threatening (from suicide), and chronic, and cause significant social, occupational, and physical dysfunction. Nearly sixty percent of all suicides are related to major depression (Broadhead, Blazer, Goerge, & Tse, 1990; El-Mallakh, Wright, Breen, & Lippmann, 1996; Pyne et al., 1997). Depressive disorders are frequently underdiagnosed and/or undertreated, for a variety of reasons

(Agency for Health Care Policy and Research, 1993). Experts say that only one-third to one-half of individuals with major depression are properly recognized by primary care physicians (Zung et al., 1993; Agency for Health Care Policy and Research, 1993).

While a number of different medications and other forms of treatment have been shown to help persons with depression, some groups of people present diagnostic and treatment challenges, for example people with chronic or recurrent depression, depression with coexisting anxiety, depression in elderly persons, and depression in people with mental retardation and other developmental disabilities.

Depression is the most common mental health disorder seen in the elderly population, but it is often difficult to diagnose because symptoms may not be classic, and affected individuals may deny many of the symptoms (Lebowitz et al., 1997). Dullness, feelings of failure, pessimism, loneliness, and hopelessness can be silent markers of underlying depression. Recent studies show, however, that healthy, normally functioning older adults seem to be at no greater risk for depression than younger adults, and what seemed to be age-related effects on depression may be due to physical health problems and related disability (Roberts, Kaplan, Shema, & Strawbridge, 1997).

Individuals with mental retardation and other developmental disabilities may present particular problems for diagnosis of depression, as well as other psychiatric disorders, because of impaired communication skills and other previously noted conditions. Matson (1983) reviewed historical attempts at making a diagnosis of depression in people with mental retardation, and noted continuing research and clinical problems related to this population. More recently, Marston and group note that diagnosis may further impaired because non-disruptive symptoms, such as increased quietness and withdrawal, may not be regarded as problems by caregivers, and thus may not be reported (Marston, Perry, & Roy, 1997). DiBartolomeo and Kaniecki (1996) have an on-going institution-based project in Apple Creek, Ohio which is attempting to diagnose this group of persons who may be too quiet. Others have reported careful attempts to separate symptoms of depression and dementia in persons with Down syndrome (Sung et al., 1997).

According to DSM-IV, for a diagnosis of depression to be made, at least five symptoms from a list of nine must have been present during the same two-week period. These symptoms must represent a change from the way the individual previously functioned, and must cause clinically significant distress or impairment of social, occupational, and/or other areas of functioning. A diagnosis cannot be made in an individual who seems to function adequately both at home and work, and during recreational activities. At least one of the five (or more) symptoms must be depressed mood or loss of interest or pleasure in daily activities (anhedonia). Depressed mood may be determined either by reports from the person himself/herself, or from observations made by others. In children, adolescents, and adults with mental retardation the mood may be irritable rather than obviously depressed (Charlot, 1997). Aggression often is a manifestation of this irritability (Lowry, 1995; Charlot, 1997). A person with mental retardation who is depressed may exhibit a sad facial expression, withdrawal, vague physical complaints, and/or regression in behavior, as well as aggression. Many people feel that anhedonia, a failure of the pleasure response, may have considerable diagnostic importance, since individuals with depression who exhibit this symptom may be more likely to respond to antidepressant drug treatment than are others (Snaith, 1993).

Other possible symptoms of depression include significant weight loss or weight gain, when not dieting, of five percent or more of body weight in a one-month period, or decrease or increase of appetite almost every day. Children who are depressed may not lose weight, but may not make expected weight gains for their gains in height. People with depression often have sleep disorders—either insomnia (not enough sleep) or hypersomnia (too much sleep)—nearly every day. Sleep disturbances in persons with mental retardation who are depressed may show up as disruptive behavior at bedtime or during the night, or excessive sleepiness during scheduled daytime activities. People with total blindness often have atypical sleep patterns associated with their blindness, and sleep abnormalities probably should not be used as one of the diagnostic criteria for depression in these individuals.

People with depression may be noted to have either increased or decreased body movement activity (psychomotor agitation or psychomotor retardation) nearly every day, as observed by others. Psychomotor agitation in a person with mental retardation may present as a behavior problem of recent onset, or worsening of a continuing behavior problem. Psychomotor retardation may show up as a change in productivity in a vocational setting. People with depression often complain of persistent fatigue or loss of energy.

People with depression frequently complain of feelings of worthlessness or excessive, inappropriate guilt. This guilt may be delusional, and does not involve merely self-reproach about being sick. Persons with mental retardation who are depressed may express these feelings in statements such as "I'm dumb—stupid—no one likes me—" (Sovner, Hurley, &

LaBrie, 1982). Persons with depression also may have decreased ability to think or concentrate, and may appear indecisive. These symptoms may be reported by the individual or by others. In persons with mental retardation, cognitive disturbances associated with depression may show up as a decrease in I.Q. or functional ability, or by change in attention span while performing their usual activities (Pary, 1997).

While almost everyone may have a fear of dying, a person with depression frequently has recurrent thoughts of death or dying, and may either think a lot about suicide, plan suicide, or make suicide attempts. Risk of suicide serves to make depression a potentially life-threatening disorder.

For a diagnosis of depression to be made, as noted above, the symptoms must cause the individual clinically significant distress, and/or must impair social, occupational, or other important areas of functioning. Symptoms due to the direct effects of a substance, such as various medications or drugs of abuse, or general medical conditions, should not be counted as criteria in making a diagnosis of major depression. A diagnosis of depression is not generally made if symptoms occur within two months of the loss of a loved one, unless symptoms are associated with marked functional impairment, morbid preoccupation with worthlessness, suicidal thoughts, symptoms of psychosis, or marked psychomotor retardation.

Bipolar I Disorder (Manic)

Questions to ask:

- Does this person talk a lot, with a real "push" of speech?
- Does this person think he/she is far more capable than he/she in reality is?
- Does this person appear to require virtually no sleep?
- Is this person more distractible and hyperactive than in earlier life?

Important clues:

- The person appears to have virtually limitless energy, and to be in constant motion.
- The behavior has not been present since early childhood.
- The behavior appears to be cyclic.

Mnemonic for Bipolar I disorder:

Very impressed with own importance—

Every night has very little, if any, sleep—

Revved-up thought processes—

Yammers or talks constantly—

Has a very short, virtually nonexistent, attention span—

Increase in goal-directed activity, or agitation—

Goes partying constantly, despite consequences—

Has no history of similar behavior very early in life—

*****

Mood disorders are common conditions that have as their main feature a disturbance in feeling. Mood disorders are divided into depressive disorders, bipolar disorders, and two disorders based on cause—general medical condition or substance-induced. Bipolar disorders have in common the presence or history of a manic episode, mixed episode, or hypomanic episode, often accompanied by the presence or history of a major depression. Bipolar I disorder, with an incidence of approximately 0.8% of the adult population (American Psychiatric Association, 1994b) is marked by one or more manic or mixed episodes, usually accompanied by episode(s) of major depression. Bipolar II disorder, with a lifetime incidence of 0.5%, is characterized by one or more episodes of major depression, accompanied by at least one hypomanic episode.

A manic episode is defined by a distinct period during which an abnormally and persistently elevated (euphoric), expansive, or irritable mood is present, lasting at least a week. The abnormal mood in a manic episode, according to DSM-IV, must be accompanied by at least three other symptoms from a list which includes inflated self-esteem or bravado, decreased need for sleep, pressure of speech, flight of ideas, distractibility, increased involvement in goal-directed and/or pleasurable activities with high risk of bad outcomes, and/or agitation. Humility and meekness are not symptoms of a manic episode.

To be considered part of a manic episode, symptoms must be severe enough to caused marked impairment in social or occupational functioning and/or to require hospitalization, or psychotic features are present. Elevated mood of a manic episode may be described as euphoric, unusually good, cheerful, or "high." While elevated mood is considered a standard symptom of a manic episode, irritability or switching back and forth between euphoria and irritability is often seen, particularly when the person's wishes are not immediately carried out.

Inflated self-esteem is usually present. This may vary from uncritical self-confidence all the way to marked grandiosity, which may appear delusional. A person in a manic episode may feel he/she is extremely important and wise, and may give advice on matters about which they know nothing. It has been said that a person without mental retardation who is manic thinks he/she is God, while a person with mental retardation who is manic thinks he/she is normal.

A person experiencing a manic episode usually has a decreased need for sleep, often awakening several hours earlier than usual, feeling full of energy, or even going for days without sleep, without feeling tired. Electroencephalographic sleep patterns show significantly decreased total time spent asleep, increased time awake in the last two hours of recording, shortened rapid eye movement (REM) latency (the time before the first REM period of the night), and increased REM activity and density (Hudson, Lipinski, Frankenburg, Grochocinski, & Kupfer, 1988).

Manic speech is usually pressured, loud, very rapid, and difficult to interrupt. A person with mania may become theatrical, with dramatic gestures and singing. Sounds rather than meaning of words may govern word choice, a process known as *clanging*. Speech may involve a lot of joking.

The person with a manic episode may have racing thoughts, often faster than can be spoken. Distractibility may show up as an inability to screen out unrelated stimuli, or to tell the difference between thoughts that pertain to the current topic or thoughts that are clearly irrelevant. The racing thoughts have been reported to feel like watching two or three television programs at the same time. Often this "flight of ideas" results in an almost continuous flow of fast speech, with sudden changes from one topic to another.

Distractibility is evidenced by an inability to screen out unimportant or irrelevant stimuli such as background noises, the color of the interviewer's tie, or room furnishings.

Increase in goal-directed activity often involves excessive planning of and participation in many different activities at the same time. Increased sexual drive, fantasies, and behavior are often present. Very often increased sociability is present, to the extent of being quite obnoxious to others. Expansiveness, unwarranted optimism, grandiosity, and poor judgement often lead to unwise involvement in pleasurable activities such as shopping sprees, reckless driving, foolish business investments, and unusual sexual behavior, even though these activities may result in harm. A person who suddenly orders twenty new suits without being able to pay for them, and begins to have numerous sexual encounters with strangers, may be having a manic episode.

According to Sovner and Hurley (1982b), in persons with mental retardation, hyperactivity is the thread connecting all of the associated symptoms of mania. They also note that the euphoric state of a person with mental retardation and mania is not as infectious as in others. One difficulty in making a diagnosis of mania in a person with any developmental disability is that many of the symptoms consistent with mania already are present. These symptoms increase in severity when the individual becomes manic. Anther confirming factor is the fact that the hyperactivity is periodic. (Caution should be observed, however, in using cyclic features as a basis for diagnosis of mood disorders. Bipolar disorders are very often cyclic, but all cyclic behavior patterns are not bipolar disorders.) Often the individual also has periods of withdrawal, sadness or depression. He/she also often has a family history of a mood disorder.

Persons with velo-cardio-facial syndrome, also known as Shprintzen syndrome, a relatively common disorder with multiple physical abnormalities, which may include learning disabilities, have an increased prevalence of early onset bipolar disorder (Papolos et al., 1996). A tendency of increased prevalence of bipolar disorder in persons with Tourette disorder has also been noted (Kerbeshian, Burd, & Klug, 1995).

A hypomanic episode is one in which symptoms are not severe enough to cause marked functional impairment or require hospitalization. Some evidence exists that people with hypomania are far more common among the corporate and professional elite, with symptoms actually representing positive characteristics for people in business (Jenkins, 1996).

A mixed episode is characterized by a period of time, lasting at least one week, in which criteria are met both for a manic episode and a major depressive episode nearly every day. The disturbance must be sufficiently severe to cause marked impairment in life or to require hospitalization.

Either type of bipolar disorder must be distinguished from episodes of a mood disorder due to a general medical condition, when episodes are the direct result of that condition. As an example, persons with multiple sclerosis often have a special risk for mood swings, not just a reaction to the stress of the medical problem, some of which involve euphoria. Sometimes a brain tumor or Cushing syndrome (excessive adrenal gland activity) may present with manic symptoms. An individual with an overactive thyroid gland may appear hypomanic. These medical conditions should always be considered in a person with new-onset symptoms, since they must be treated appropriately. Some substances, such as drugs of abuse, medications, or exposure to a toxin, cause manic symptoms. Symptoms similar to those in mania may be secondary to cocaine or amphetamines. Manic symptoms also may result from treatment of depression with medication, electroconvulsive therapy, or light therapy.

Symptoms of major depression with prominent irritable mood may be difficult to distinguish from manic episodes with irritable mood or from mixed episodes. Attention-deficit/hyperactivity disorder and a manic episode are both marked by excessive activity, impulsive behavior, poor judgement, and denial of problems. Attention-deficit/hyperactivity disorder is distinguished from a manic episode by its early onset (before age seven), chronic rather than off-and-on course, and absence of abnormally elevated or expansive mood or psychotic features.

Anxiety Disorders

Questions to ask:

- Does this person seem to be nervous and fearful?
- Does this person appear to have frequent spells of rapid pulse, sweating, shaking, and/or complain of chest pain?
- Does this person seem dizzy, unsteady, or "fainty?"

Important clues:

- The person has many health complaints which aren't really accompanied by objective findings.
- The person keeps his/her back to the wall when in a group.
- The person has many repetitive behaviors and routines which seem to make him/her feel better.
- The person has a history of severe psychic and/or physical trauma.

Mnemonic for panic attack:

Very "trembly" or "shaky"—

Extra fast, hard heart beats—

Rather sweaty—

Yucky feelings of choking, shortness of breath, and/or smothering—

Nausea or abdominal pain—

Even has chest pain or discomfort—

Really has feelings of numbness or tingling—

Very dizzy, unsteady, lightheaded, or faint—

Often has feelings of unreality or being detached from self—

Underlying fears of losing control, going crazy, and/or being about to die—

So very chilly or so very flushed—

*****

Anxiety disorders are the most common mental health disorders seen by primary care physicians. The typical primary care physician sees at least one patient with an anxiety disorder every day (McGlynn & Metcalf, 1989). Anxiety disorders seem to be about twice as common in women as in men, affecting as many as one-third of all women at some time during their life (Zoler, 1995). Studies show that only 23% of people who meet criteria for having an anxiety disorder have received any sort of treatment (Leaman, 1993). While reports concerning the overall rate of anxiety disorders in persons with mental retardation are conflicting (Reiss, 1994), in a study of 251 institutionalized persons with severe or profound mental retardation referred for psychiatric assessment, King and group (1994) found that 12% of the individuals had collections of signs and symptoms that were best considered as part of the anxiety disorder spectrum.

Characteristic features of this group of disorders include symptoms of anxiety and avoidance behavior. While depression and anxiety disorders have some symptoms in common, and may occur in the same person, features more characteristic of anxiety include difficulty falling asleep, avoidance based on fear, rapid pulse, breathing difficulties, feeling of dread, tremors, heart palpitations, sweating, hot or cold spells, and dizziness. Another symptom often associated with anxiety disorders is the feeling of detachment from all or parts of one's body, depersonalization. Derealization, another frequently associated symptom, is the sensation that the immediate environment is strange, unreal, or unfamiliar (McGlynn & Metcalf, 1989).

A panic attack can occur in a variety of anxiety disorders, usually providing a common diagnostic thread between disorders, but not representing a diagnosis in itself. A panic attack is a group of symptoms which occur during a distinct period of intense fear or discomfort. DSM-IV lists 13 of these symptoms, four of which must be present, develop suddenly, and reach a peak within ten minutes. Among listed symptoms of a panic attack are heart palpitations, sweating, trembling or shaking, shortness of breath or sensation of smothering, feeling of choking, chest pain or discomfort, and nausea or abdominal distress. Some of the symptoms of a panic attack, such as palpitations, shortness of breath, and chest pain, may be mistaken for a heart attack. Forty percent of people with panic attacks never seek care for their attacks, but those who do usually use medical rather than mental health settings (Katerndahl & Realini, 1995). One recent study (Katerndahl & Trammell, 1997) found that about one half of 51 patients presenting with a new complaint of chest pain met criteria for either panic disorder or infrequent panic, but few physicians recognized the panic state.

Other listed symptoms of a panic attack include feeling dizzy or lightheaded, derealization (feelings of unreality) or depersonalization (feeling detached from one's self), fear of losing control or going crazy, fear of dying, paresthesias (numbness or tingling sensations), and chills or hot flushes.

The term *agoraphobia* means anxiety about being in places or situations from which escape might be difficult or embarrassing, or where help might not be available in the event of having an unexpected panic attack. Panic attacks may occur with or without agoraphobia.

Other conditions such as the effects of some prescribed drugs, drugs of abuse, or overactive thyroid gland may present with symptoms similar to the symptoms of a panic attack, and should, of course, be carefully ruled out.

a) Panic Disorder

To make a diagnosis of panic disorder without agoraphobia, periodic, unexpected panic attacks must be present, and at least one attack should be followed by a month or more of persistent concern about having more attacks, worry about the significance of the attack or its consequences, and/or a significant behavior change related to the attacks. Panic disorder often causes significant functional disability (Hollifield et al., 1997). Panic disorder with or without agoraphobia probably is fairly common. Charles Darwin (1809-1882), while traveling widely throughout the world in pursuit of scientific explorations, suffered from a chronic illness marked by severe symptoms of anxiety. These problems impaired his functioning and severely limited his activities (Barloon & Noyes, 1997).

Panic disorder accounts for more emergency department visits than any other psychiatric illness, with up to 28% of persons with panic symptoms presenting to that department, since persons in the midst of a panic attack often believe they are about to die (Rosenbaum, 1996). Panic disorder is estimated to occur five times as often in people with asthma than in the general population ("Patients can confuse," 1997). While both panic disorder and asthma can have symptoms referable to breathing, wheezing is a symptom of asthma and not of panic attack (Schmaling & Bell, 1997).

While panic disorder is said to be virtually unreported in persons with mental retardation (Khreim & Mikkelsen, 1997), at least three case reports have relatively recently appeared (Loschen & Saliga, 2000; Khreim & Mikkelsen, 1996; Malloy, Zealberg, & Paolone, 1998).

b) Phobias

A specific phobia is defined as a distinct and persistent fear of a specific object or situation. Examples include fear of flying, heights, animals, receiving an injection, and seeing blood. Exposure to the specific object or situation almost always causes an immediate anxiety response, which often takes the form of a panic attack, which is determined by or predisposed to the situation.

In children, panic associated with a phobia may be expressed by crying, tantrums, freezing, or clinging. Persons with mental retardation may react in similar ways, or may become aggressive to get away from the feared situation. People with mental retardation probably are vulnerable to the full range of phobias (Szymanski et al., 1998). Adults with phobias recognize that the fear is excessive or unreasonable, but this feature may be absent in persons with mental retardation or in children.

In a true phobia, the avoidance, anxious anticipation, and/or distress in the feared situations interfere significantly with normal routine, functioning, social activities, or relationships with others, or there is marked distress about having the phobia. Relatively trivial fears about flying, involving only the tight gripping of armrests on takeoff and landing, do not meet criteria for a phobic disorder.

c) Generalized Anxiety Disorder

Many people with anxiety have generalized anxiety disorder, in which they have excessive anxiety and worry about a number of events or activities, occurring more days than not, for at least six months. The individual with generalized anxiety disorder finds to difficult to control his/her worry. Associated symptoms may include restlessness, susceptibility to fatigue, difficulty concentrating, irritability, muscle tension, and sleep disturbance. Sleep disturbances may involve trouble falling asleep or staying asleep, or restless, unsatisfying sleep. The anxiety, worry, and/or physical symptoms of generalized anxiety disorder cause significant problems in social, occupational, or other important areas of functioning. Some medications, such as those used to treat asthma, can cause symptoms similar to generalized anxiety disorder, as do some general medical conditions, such as over-active thyroid gland.

d) Obsessive Compulsive Disorder

Obsessive compulsive disorder (OCD) is an anxiety disorder in which obsessions and/or compulsions must be present. Obsessions are defined as recurrent and persistent thoughts, impulses, or images that are experienced, at some time during the disturbance, as distracting and inappropriate, and cause marked anxiety and/or distress. Thoughts, impulses, or images associated with obsessions are not simply excessive worries about real-life problems. The affected individual attempts to ignore or suppress these thoughts or images, or tries to neutralize them with some other thought or action.

A person with OCD recognizes that the obsessional thoughts, impulses, or images are a product of his/her own mind, and not imposed from without. Children or persons with mental retardation may not realize that the obsessional thoughts come from within. (A person who feels that he must wash his hands continuously because God is telling him he is unclean does not meet criteria for OCD, since he perceives the commands as coming from outside himself/herself.)

Compulsions are defined as repeated behaviors, such as handwashing, ordering, checking, or mental acts, such as praying or counting, that the person feels drive to perform in response to an obsession, or according to rigid rules. These rules or behaviors are aimed at preventing or reducing distress or preventing some dreaded event or situation, but are not connected in a realistic way to that distress, or are excessive.

At some point during the course of OCD, the person has recognized that the obsessions and/or compulsions are excessive or unreasonable. This standard does not necessarily apply to children or persons with mental retardation. The obsessions and/or compulsions cause marked distress, are time-consuming (more than an hour a day), and may markedly interfere with the person's normal routine and quality of life (Calvocoressi, Libman, Vegso, McDougle, & Price, 1998).

While some experts note that, since OCD in the general population is felt to be associated with above average intelligence, relatively low rates of OCD should be expected in persons with mental retardation (Reiss, 1994), others suspect that OCD may be more prevalent in persons with mental retardation than in the general population (Vitiello & Behar, 1992). Gedye (1996) feels that recent accounts of dramatic increases in prevalence rates of OCD in groups of people with mental retardation are indicative of the earlier lack of recognition of the form that OCD can take in this population as compared to the general population. She cites a study of her own of 50 adults with developmental disabilities who met criteria for OCD according to her examination. In this group more than 90% had never previously been diagnosed with this disorder.

Gedye (1996) has developed the Compulsive Behavior Checklist for use with people with developmental disabilities. This instrument lists 25 types of compulsions "done" by adults with developmental disabilities. This checklist does not make a diagnosis of OCD, but was designed for use by consultants in interviewing staff members, or others who know the affected persons well. The 25 types of compulsions are grouped into five categories: ordering compulsions, completeness/incompleteness compulsions, cleaning/tidiness compulsions, checking/touching compulsions, and deviant grooming compulsions.

Ordering compulsions include arranging objects in certain patterns, arranging items in one spot, wanting chairs in a fixed arrangement, wanting/arranging peers to sit in certain chairs, using the same chair or location when in a particular room, and insisting on doing a certain activity at the same time of day.

Completeness/incompleteness compulsions include insisting on closing open doors, taking all items out of a storage area, removing items and then returning them, over and over, trying to empty all toiletry bottles in the bathroom, putting on and taking off clothing over and over, and insisting on doing a certain chore, without letting anyone else do it.

Cleaning/tidiness compulsions include insisting on doing personal hygiene steps in a fixed sequence, cleaning body parts excessively, insisting on picking up stray bits from the ground, picking at loose threads continuously, ripping clothes if not prevented, insisting that a certain activity be done, and hiding or hoarding particular objects.

Checking/touching compulsions include opening a cupboard door and then reclosing it, over and over, touching or tapping an item repeatedly, going through a touching or stepping pattern, or doing unusual sniffing. (Some people with autism appear to go through some of these same rituals.)

Deviant grooming compulsions include picking at face, hands, legs, or other body parts, to the extent of gouging skin, checking self in a mirror excessively, inappropriate hair cutting, pulling at hair, and pulling out hair when sitting calmly.

After some count of the types of compulsions and the number of categories of obsessions exhibited by a person with mental retardation, some assessment of the amount of interference with daily living should be made, particularly whether or not the compulsions take more than an hour each day if not prevented, and whether or not they significantly interfere with the person's normal routine.

Another important part of the Compulsive Behavior Checklist involves a measure of the response of the involved individual to interruption of the compulsive behaviors by others. Examples include halting momentarily, then resuming the activity, waiting until the observer is gone, then resuming, becoming angry and aggressive against whoever intervenes, biting or hitting self, or headbanging.

e) Posttraumatic Stress Disorder

Post-traumatic stress disorder (PTSD) is an anxiety disorder in which the involved person has been exposed to a traumatic event in which he/she has experienced, witnessed, or been confronted with a situation involving actual or threatened death or serious injury, to self and/or others. The individual's response to this event must have involved intense fear, helplessness, or horror. In PTSD the traumatic event is persistently re-experienced in recurrent and intrusive recollections of the event, recurrent distressing dreams of the event, acting or feeling as if the event were recurring, very severe psychological distress in response to cues symbolizing the event, and/or physical symptoms on exposure to cues/reminders of the event.

Persons with PTSD persistently avoid stimuli associated with the trauma, and seem to have numbing of general sensitivity. These symptoms may present as efforts to avoid thoughts, feelings, or conversations associated with the trauma, efforts to avoid situations or people that cause memories of the trauma, and/or inability to recall details about the trauma. Other evidences of PTSD may include decreased interest or participation in significant activities, feelings of detachment or estrangement from others, inability to have loving feelings, and/or a sense of not expecting to have a normal life span.

People with PTSD have persistent symptoms of increased arousal, such as trouble falling or staying asleep, irritability or outbursts of anger, trouble concentrating, hypervigilance, and perhaps exaggerated startle response. An individual with mental retardation who always keeps his back to the wall when he is in a room with others, and watches everyone around very closely, has the symptom of hypervigilance.

To make a diagnosis of post-traumatic stress disorder, the duration of the disturbance must be more than one month, and the disturbance must cause significant distress or impairment in important areas of functioning. In persons with mental retardation, sometimes the obstacle to recognition and documentation of criteria of PTSD is resistance of those close to the person to the idea that such horrible things could occur, particularly things that may be perpetrated against people unable to defend themselves (Ryan, 2000). If an individual has occasional bad dreams about an auto accident, but otherwise seems alright, he/she probably does not have PTSD.

Psychotic Disorders

Questions to ask:

- Does this person seem to see or hear things that are not there?
- How do you know?

Important clues:

- The person sees or hears things that are not there, and—
- The person does not have bipolar disorder.

Mnemonic for some symptoms/features of psychosis:

Pretty strange ideas, not based in reality (delusions)—

Seeing/hearing things that are not there (hallucinations)-

Yes, symptoms may vary over time—

Catatonic or grossly disorganized behavior—

Has "negative" symptoms such as flat affect, lack of movement—

Other conditions, such as mood disorders with psychotic features, have been ruled out—

Speech disorganized, perhaps incoherent—

Interference with social/occupational function—

Signs of the disturbance have persisted at least six months, with at least one month of active symptoms—

*****

The term psychosis has been defined a number of different ways, but very strictly includes only conditions which include delusions and/or prominent hallucinations. Delusions are incorrect beliefs that usually involve a misinterpretation of perceptions or experiences. As an example, if an individual firmly believes that his/her thoughts are controlled by a special radio in his/her head, that person is said to have a delusion. Hallucinations are experienced as hearing, seeing, smelling, tasting, or touching something which is not there. Auditory (hearing) hallucinations are by far the most common type, and are characteristic of schizophrenia. To be considered a symptom of psychosis, hallucinations must occur in the framework of a clear sensorium—the affected individual cannot be just falling asleep or just waking up, or under the influence of some sort of mind-altering chemical/drug.

Persons with psychosis usually have very disorganized thinking. Since virtually the only way to know what a person is thinking is through what that person says about those thoughts, disorganization of speech should be carefully assessed. Since mildly disorganized speech is common, to be counted as a symptom the disorganization must be obviously severe, and interfere with normal communication.

Disorganized behavior associated with psychosis may manifest itself in a variety of ways, ranging from childish silliness to unpredictable agitation. Problems may be noted in any form of goal-directed behavior, leading to difficulties in performing activities of daily living, such as organizing meals or maintaining personal hygiene. Grossly disorganized behavior must be distinguished from behavior that is just aimless or generally unpurposeful, and from organized behavior prompted by delusional beliefs. Also, occasional episodes of restless, angry, or agitated behavior shouldn't be considered as evidence of psychosis, especially if the motivation is understandable.

Catatonic motor behaviors include a marked decrease in reaction to the environment, sometimes reaching the extreme unawareness of catatonic stupor, maintaining a rigid posture and resisting efforts to be moved (catatonic rigidity), and/or assuming bizarre postures. Catatonic symptoms are nonspecific, and may occur in other mental disorders such as mood disorders.

While positive symptoms such as hallucinations and/or delusions may be dramatic, negative symptoms of schizophrenia and other psychotic disorders, such as affective flattening, alogia (inability to speak), and avolition (inability to make a decision) may also be very disabling. Affective flattening is common, and is marked by the individual's face looking immobile and unresponsive, with poor eye contact and reduced body language. Negative symptoms are hard to evaluate because they are nonspecific, perhaps appearing just more severe than normal behaviors, and may be due to a variety of things other than psychosis.

Some medication side effects may look quite like negative symptoms of psychosis. The distinction between true negative symptoms and medication side effects depends on clinical judgement, particularly assessment of the severity of the negative symptoms, the nature and type of medication, the effects of dosage adjustment, and the effect(s) of other medications. Negative symptoms of psychosis may look very much like symptoms of depression, except people with depression are sad and uncomfortable, while people with psychosis appear more "empty" of feelings. Also, on occasion people learn to be withdrawn, if they live in a very unstimulating environment.

For a diagnosis of psychosis to be made, several symptoms must be present together for at least a month, and some signs of disturbance must persist continuously for at least six months. Often less severe symptoms are present before the active phase of the condition, prodromal symptoms, and some symptoms may persist after the active phase, residual symptoms.

Accurate diagnosis of psychosis in persons with mental retardation is difficult, but not impossible, particularly since the presence of hallucinations and/or delusions usually is determined by self-report, and many people with mental retardation have problems with communication (Silka & Hauser, 1997). Also, behaviors often seen in persons with moderate or more severe mental retardation may be easily confused with behavioral deficits associated with schizophrenia. Examples include stereotypic behaviors, self-stimulatory behavior, and lack of appropriate social interactions. Distinguishing between hallucinations and delusions, and other, less serious, symptoms, is quite important in establishing an effective treatment program for persons with mental retardation. A person with mental retardation who has hallucinations is more likely to have depression or a significant life stressor than to have schizophrenia (Charlot, 1997). Although a mental health interview may seem rather simple, the ability to be specific, report feelings and abstractions, time frame of symptoms, and history is severely limited in persons with mental retardation. Often, due to a process of diagnostic overshadowing, every abnormal behavior may be attributed to the mental retardation, and mental health problems may actually be ignored (Reiss, 1994). Sometimes, instead of missing a psychiatric disorder, when assessing persons with mental retardation for behavior difficulties, a clinician may see the problem as a psychotic disorder and perhaps prescribe antipsychotic drugs, in a form of diagnostic distortion. In this instance situational problems, depression, anxiety disorders, and other mental health problems may be missed, and treatment prescribed for the wrong disorder.

During the course of normal development young children often talk to themselves, engage in solitary fantasy play, or invent imaginary friends. These behaviors are also typical of many adults with mental retardation who do not have mental illness. Persons with mental retardation often have many sorrows and disappointments during their lives. Repeated failures and rejections may lead to the development of self-gratifying fantasies, which may resemble delusions. Any delusions in persons with mental retardation should first be considered as possible fantasy, which may be made worse by unmet need and stress.

Sometimes hallucinations and delusions appear in persons in the normal population who aren't psychotic, and certainly this may also happen in persons with mental retardation. Everyone who assesses a person with mental retardation and apparent psychotic symptoms should consider stress as the most likely explanation for such behavior. Additional information may be obtained from a check of changes in mood and sleep. Many experts feel that, in a confusing picture with complex presentation, psychosis should be intentionally underdiagnosed, since psychotic disorder is much less common than mood disorders in persons with mental retardation.

Personality Disorders

Questions to ask:

- Does this person seem to have a peculiar way of thinking and/or looking at the world?
- Has he/she always been this way?
- Does this person have more frequent or less frequent than the usual mood swings?
- Has he/she always been this way?
- Do most people consider this person odd?

- Has this always been the case?

Important clues:

- The person has, and has had for many years, an enduring pattern of behavior and apparent inner experience that differs markedly from that of their culture.

*****

A personality disorder is an enduring pattern of inner experience and behavior that is markedly different from the affected individual's culture. Every person is different from every other person, whether or not they have developmental disabilities. When those differences cause distress or damage to social, occupational, or other important areas of functioning, then a personality disorder is said to be present. An individual who seems peculiar, but who functions relatively well at work, at home, and in the community probably doesn't have a personality disorder. He/she may have a peculiar personality type, but no personality disorder is present. People with different cultural backgrounds are apt to act in different ways. Behavior that appears peculiar to the dominant culture but which is part of the individual's culture is not a symptom of a personality disorder. Personality disorders are rather common in the general population, with one study indicating a 5.9% incidence, with 9.3% incidence when provisional cases were included (Samuels, Nestadt, Romanoski, Folstein, & McHugh, 1994).

The pattern of a personality disorder is manifested in at least two of a list of areas involving cognition, affectivity, interpersonal functioning, and impulse control. Cognition refers to ways of perceiving and interpreting self, other people and events. Affectivity refers to the range, intensity, instability, and appropriateness of emotional response.

The enduring patterns of personality disorders are inflexible and pervasive across a broad range of personal and social situations. Patterns associated with personality disorders are stable and of long duration, with onset usually as far back as adolescence or early adulthood. When state disorders are defined as conditions which are relatively short, with a beginning and usually an ending, and trait disorders are considered more pervasive and of long duration, personality disorders can be said to be trait disorders (Widiger & Frances, 1988).

The ten classified personality disorders in *Diagnostic and Statistical Manual of Mental Disorders, Fourth Edition* (American Psychiatric Association, 1994a) are often grouped into three clusters as 1) Odd or eccentric (paranoid, schizoid, and schizotypal), 2) Dramatic, emotional or erratic (antisocial, borderline, histrionic, and narcissistic), and 3) Anxious or fearful (avoidant, dependent, and obsessive compulsive). As an example, an individual with a long-term history of dramatic, emotional, and unpredictable behavior may have a personality disorder, which is apt to include narcissistic, histrionic, antisocial, and/or borderline personality disorders. Many persons can be diagnosed with more than one personality disorder (Shea, 1995).

Individuals with schizoid personality disorder often appear peculiar. They seem to be detached from social relationships, and have a narrow range of expression of emotions in interpersonal settings. These symptoms begin by early adulthood, and are present in a variety of settings. For a diagnosis of schizoid personality disorder to be made, the individual must demonstrate at least four of seven listed symptoms, including lack of desire for or enjoyment of close relationships, including family, choice of solitary activities, little interest in sexual experiences, lack of pleasure in most activities, and lack of close friends. Other symptoms may include apparent indifference to the praise or criticism of others, and emotional coldness, detachment, or "flattened" affectivity.

Individuals with schizotypal personality disorder share with schizoid personality disorder reduced ability to make close relationships. They are often quite uncomfortable with close relationships, and often have odd beliefs or magical thinking, which may influence their behavior. These beliefs are not consistent with what is considered normal in their culture. People with schizotypal personality disorder frequently are extremely suspicious of others, and appear emotionally "flat." They often lack close friends, and have a lot of anxiety in social situations. This anxiety tends to be associated with paranoid fears rather than with negative judgement about their own capabilities. An individual who functions relatively well in his/her daily life, but has a strong belief in clairvoyance, telepathy, or "sixth sense," probably doesn't have a schizotypal personality disorder.

To be diagnosed as having antisocial personality disorder, an individual must be at least 18 years old, and must have shown a pervasive pattern of disregard for and violation of the rights of others, with symptoms occurring since before the age of 15. An individual who gets into the drug culture at 19 after a rather uneventful earlier life probably shouldn't be diagnosed as having an antisocial personality disorder. A person with antisocial personality disorder fails to conform to norms of society with respect to lawful behaviors, as indicated by repeatedly performing acts that are grounds for arrest. People with this disorder often are well-known to law enforcement officials, since they usually are repeat offenders. Impulsivity, failure to plan ahead, irritability, aggressiveness, and reckless disregard for the safety of self or others may all be symptoms of antisocial personality disorder. People with this condition frequently get into physical fights or commit physical assaults. Consistent irresponsibility associated with antisocial personality disorder usually is manifested by failure to sustain consistent work behavior or honor financial obligations. Individuals with this disorder show a lack of remorse, and appear indifferent to hurting, mistreating, or stealing from others. An individual who repeatedly lies, uses aliases, and "cons" others for personal profit or pleasure, then pretends to be sorry for his/her misdeeds and promises to reform, but doesn't do so, may have an antisocial personality disorder. A man who has mild mental retardation and is arrested for storing stolen merchandise for family members in his agency-furnished apartment probably doesn't have antisocial personality disorder, since he serves a useful, if illegal and unfortunate, function in his cultural environment. He is important to his family.

*****

Mnemonic for borderline personality disorder:

So frantic about avoiding abandonment—

Overvaluing, alternating with undervaluing, others—

Unstable self-image or sense of self—

Not prudent about activities that can be self-damaging, such as spending, sex, substance abuse, reckless driving, binge eating—

Self-mutilating or suicidal behavior, often recurrent—

Too moody, but quickly up and down—

All sorts of empty feelings—

Bouts of anger, temper tantrums—

Lack of control—

Episodes of temporary paranoia and/or dissociation—

*****

The essential feature of borderline personality disorder is a pervasive pattern of instability of self-image, interpersonal relationships, and mood. Borderline personality disorder is often accompanied by many features of other personality disorders. Persons with this condition often appear "contrary" in social situations, and have a generally pessimistic outlook on life. They appear to alternate between desires for dependency and self-assertion. During periods of extreme stress they may have temporary symptoms of psychosis, but these are not usually severe enough to treat with medication. Borderline personality disorder is apparently rather common in the general population.

Persons with borderline personality disorder often make frantic efforts to avoid real or imagined abandonment. Their interpersonal relationships are frequently marked by alternating between idealization and devaluation. They seem to either hate or love people, with these emotions changing frequently, even toward the same person. They have markedly and very persistently unstable self-image or sense of self. Persons with borderline personality disorder frequently are impulsive in their behavior. To count as a diagnostic factor this must involve at least two areas that are potentially self-damaging, such as sex, spending, substance abuse, reckless driving, and binge eating. An individual with impulsive behavior that is trivial and usually just involves talking too rashly does not have this criterion for a diagnosis of borderline personality disorder.

People with borderline personality disorder may have recurrent suicidal behavior, gestures, and/or threats, or may exhibit self-mutilating behavior. A person who picks continuously at his/her skin until bleeding occurs is exhibiting self-mutilating behavior. While self-injurious behavior (SIB) sometimes is a symptom of borderline personality disorder, persons with mental retardation and SIB must have other symptoms of borderline personality disorder before a diagnosis can be made.

Individuals with borderline personality disorder often have mood instability, with frequent "ups and downs." Episodes of unhappiness, irritability, or anxiety usually last a few hours, and rarely ever more than a few days. These episodes may, however, occur very frequently. People with this disorder usually don't have periods of sadness that last for months without remission.

Symptoms of borderline personality in persons with mental retardation appear to be quite similar to those in the general population (Hurley & Sovner, 1988).

While classified by DSM-IV under the category of dissociative disorder rather than personality disorder, dissociative identity disorder, formerly called multiple personality disorder, does on occasion occur, even in people with developmental disabilities. A full-blown clinical picture of dissociative identity disorder probably is quite rare in this population. Diagnostic criteria include the presence of two or more distinct identities or personality states, each with its own relatively enduring pattern. The identities or personality states recurrently take control of the person's behavior, and the individual is unable to recall important personal information. This problem with recall is too extensive to be explained by ordinary forgetfulness. Careful attempts should be made in children, and probably in persons with mental retardation, to avoid attributing the symptoms of imaginary playmates or other fantasy play to the presence of more than one personality.

e) Medical/Drug-induced Disorders

Questions to ask:

- Does the individual have a known health problem that is causing these symptoms/this behavior?
- Does the individual have a previously unrecognized health problem that is causing this behavior?
- Does this individual take medication?
- Is this a new medication?
- Has he/she had an increase in dosage of a medication?
- Is the individual undergoing a neuroleptic drug taper?
- Is the individual blind?
- Might the individual have a primary sleep disorder that may be causing the behavior?
- Does the person have strange muscle jerks or make strange noises without apparent reason?

Important clues:

- The person has a health problem which may be causing discomfort or distress.
- The person has received a new medication or increased dosage of an old medication.
- The person is undergoing a neuroleptic drug withdrawal.
- The person has a primary sleep disorder.
- The person has evidence of a tic disorder.

*****

When a new behavior problem develops in an individual who is receiving any kind of medication, particularly a new medication or increased dosage of an old medication, some kind of medication reaction should be suspected. No medication is completely without side effects. An undesirable side effect in one individual may be the desired drug effect in another (Wood, 1994). Some drug reactions are idiosyncratic (unique to the individual), some are dose-related, and some are both. An idiosyncratic reaction occurs because of something specific to the person himself/herself. Everyone who receives a particular medication does not have the same chance of having an adverse idiosyncratic reaction. A dose-related drug reaction is one which occurs in virtually everyone, if a large enough dosage is received. Many drugs can cause both idiosyncratic and dose-related reactions (Nies, 2001).

When neuroleptic (antipsychotic) drugs are introduced, or dosages are increased, akathisia may develop. The term akathisia refers to strong subjective feelings of distress or discomfort, frequently referred to the legs. The affected individual has a compelling need to be in constant movement, and feels required to get up and walk or continuously move around. Unfortunately akathisia is often mistaken for agitation. The distinction between akathisia and agitation is essential, since agitation might be treated with an increase in dosage, which would be expected to make the akathisia symptoms worse (Baldessarini, 2001). Akathisia appears to be largely a dose-related reaction, since symptoms usually lessen when dosage is decreased, but some people seem to be more apt to develop this drug side effect than are others.

Recent studies seem to indicate a link between high doses of high-potency (strong) neuroleptic drugs, akathisia, and violent behavior. Since many persons with developmental disabilities who are violent are given drugs of this sort, sometimes in high dosage, this is an issue of particular concern for persons charged with developing and monitoring treatment programs. Neuroleptic-induced akathisia should be carefully sought in any individual being treated with high doses of high-potency neuroleptics, but particularly in those persons with a history of aggression (Volavka, 1995; Barnes, 1992). Diagnosis of akathisia may be quite difficult in persons with mental retardation who have poor communication skills. Input from direct support staff and others who know the person well is of vital importance in making a diagnosis. A rating scale for drug-induced akathisia was described by Barnes in 1989, the objective portion of which may be helpful in assessing persons with mental retardation.

While administration of neuroleptic drugs may cause behaviorally described conditions such as akathisia, when neuroleptic drug dosages are decreased, no matter how slowly, significant withdrawal symptoms may occur (Gualtieri, Quade, Hicks, Mayo, & Schroeder, 1984; Poindexter, 1994; Baumeister, Sevin, & King, 1998). Neuroleptic withdrawal symptoms may include withdrawal dyskinesias, nausea, vomiting, poor appetite, weight loss, cold sweats, and withdrawal-related acute behavioral deterioration. Any of these symptoms may be very severe in some people, requiring dosage increase. Behavioral problems related to drug withdrawal may present as conditions previously unreported, such as sleep disorders. Behavior may differ markedly from behavior that was being "treated" with the neuroleptic drug, or previously masked psychotic symptoms may occur. These withdrawal symptoms may be more common in persons with mental retardation or others with some degree of brain damage. Weight loss is frequently problematic, with one large group study (Poindexter, 1994) showing measurable weight loss in almost 80% of 141 adults undergoing neuroleptic tapering, despite an exceptionally slow taper regimen. Many of these individuals were receiving relatively low neuroleptic dosages at the time of the taper, and almost all were relatively slender at the time, since almost 90% had body weights under the mean Body Mass Index for the U.S. population as a whole.

When benzodiazepine drugs, commonly prescribed for anxiety, are administered, some individuals show a marked disinhibiting reaction (Werry, 1998), which worsens when dosages are increased. This condition is said to be rare, but probably occurs more commonly in people with some sort of brain damage. Disinhibiting reactions due to this class drugs are probably both dose-related and idiosyncratic. Individuals who develop disinhibition to one of the benzodiazepine drugs will probably also have problems with other drugs in the same category.

Some drugs used for epilepsy have marked behavioral side effects, both in adults and children. Barbiturate anticonvulsants such as phenobarbital and primidone may have marked adverse effects on behavior, particularly irritability, aggression, and lack of cooperation (Vining et al., 1987; Hanzel, Kalachnik, & Harder, 1992; Poindexter, Berglund, & Kolstoe, 1993).

Often medication not intended for treatment of behavioral/psychiatric problems has significant behavioral side effects. As an example, DSM-IV provides a list of medications reported to cause symptoms of anxiety which includes anesthetics and analgesics, sympathomimetics or other bronchodilators (such as contained in many medications for asthma), anticholinergics, insulin, thyroid preparations, birth control pills, antihistamines, medications used to treat Parkinson's disease, corticosteroids, drugs used to treat hypertension and heart problems, anticonvulsants, lithium, antipsychotic drugs, and antidepressants (p.441). Other medications may have side effects of depression, including antihypertensives such as propranolol, barbiturate drugs such as phenobarbital, and corticosteroids. These drug side effects may be particularly problematic in persons with mental retardation, or others with communication problems, including elderly persons.

While fatigue due some sort of sleep disorder would be expected to result in behavioral difficulties, particularly in persons with mental retardation, such persons with blindness are prone to develop a circadian rhythm sleep disorder which presents particular diagnostic problems. Like most other living creatures, people have prominent daily body rhythms (circadian rhythms). Circadian rhythm is a major determiner of sleep tendency. While internal body pacemakers that set most circadian rhythms run slightly longer than 24 hours (Plumlee, 1986), melatonin, a natural substance released by the pineal gland, is released in response to light transmission from the retina of the eye, moving the body rhythms to a 24-hour pattern. This regulatory mechanisms is absent in many people with no light perception, predisposing them to a cyclic sleep disorder, since their internal mechanisms may be indicating that they should be asleep when they need to be awake, or vice versa. This problem may be more evident in persons with associated mental retardation (Poindexter & Bihm, 1994).

Several disorders considered both neurologic and psychiatric should also be considered in assessment of behavioral difficulties, particularly in persons with mental retardation. Tourette disorder is a condition that begins between the ages of two and 15 years. Persons with this condition have multiple involuntary muscular and vocal tics, (movements or sounds), with symptoms changing in frequency very slowly. Tourette disorder is fairly common, occurring in three to five persons per 10,000 in the general population (Hyde & Weinberger, 1995). It is more common in males than in females, and although the tics usually persist throughout life, they may decrease in severity and frequency after puberty. While Tourette disorder has only rarely been reported in persons with mental retardation, it probably is easily overlooked because these individuals often have stereotyped movements and peculiar vocalizations (Crews, Bonaventura, Hay, Steele, & Rowe, 1993; Rosenquist, 2000; Rosenquist & Bodfish, 1997).

Attention-deficit hyperactivity disorder (ADHD) is a common condition occurring in an estimated three to nine percent of children in North America (Taylor, 1997). Until recently experts felt that ADHD "burned itself out" by adolescence, but much evidence now indicates that ADHD can persist into adulthood (Shaffer, 1994; Feifel; 1996). One study (Hill

& Schoener, 1996) indicates that the rate of ADHD in a given age group appears to decline by 50% approximately every five years. If a prevalence rate of ADHD in childhood is assumed to be four percent, and the exponential decline is extrapolated, the estimated rate of adult ADHD ranges from about 0.8% at age 20 to 0.05% at age 40.

According to DSM-IV, symptoms of ADHD may involve either inattention or hyperactivity-impulsivity. Six or more symptoms must be present in either category for the diagnosis to be confirmed. A person with the inattentive form of ADHD has at least six symptoms from a list that includes often failing to pay attention to details or making careless mistakes in schoolwork or work, often having difficulty sustaining attention in tasks or play activities, often not seeming to listen when spoken to directly, failure to follow through on instructions, difficulty organizing tasks and activities, and avoidance of tasks that require sustained mental effort. Other possible symptoms include often losing things necessary for tasks or activities, easy distractibility, and forgetfulness in daily activities.

An individual with the hyperactive-impulsive form of ADHD has at least six symptoms from a list in DSM-IV that includes often fidgeting with hands or feet or squirming in the seat, leaving seat when expected to stay seated, often moving around a lot in situations where this is not appropriate, often being unable to engage in any activity quietly, and talking excessively. Other symptoms may include the appearance of being "on the go" all of the time, difficulty waiting his/her turn, often blurting out answers to questions before the questions are completed, and often intruding on or interrupting other people.

A diagnosis of ADHD cannot be made unless symptoms causing significant impairment were present before age seven, and unless some impairment is present in at least two different settings.

Like their childhood counterparts, adults with ADHD have difficulty modulating attention. They have problems staying focused for any but the briefest time intervals, particularly when tasks are low key, without much variety. Unfortunately, children and adults who are inattentive but not hyperactive are less likely to be recognized as possibly having ADHD than are those who are hyperactive. Even when hyperactivity is present during childhood, it is the most likely symptom to disappear with age. Many experts feel that mood disturbance is a common feature of ADHD in adults.

Diagnosis of ADHD in people with developmental disabilities is often difficult, particularly in persons with more severe cognitive disabilities, who may have hyperactivity or overactivity because of diffuse brain dysfunction rather than ADHD. Several medical disorders cause symptoms resembling those of ADHD, including thyroid and other endocrine disorders, fatigue syndromes, and some neurologic disorders. The cause of ADHD is unknown, but some genetic factor seems to be involved, since the disorder often seems to "run" in families (Taylor, 1997).

REFERENCES

Agency for Health Care Policy and Research. (1993). *Depression in primary care: Volume 1. Detection and diagnosis* (AHCPR Publication No. 93-0550). Washington, DC: U.S. Government Printing Office.

American Academy of Pediatrics. (1996). *The classification of child and adolescent mental diagnoses in primary care: Diagnostic and statistical manual for primary care (DSM-PC) child and adolescent version.* Elk Grove Village, IL: Author.

American Psychiatric Association. (1994a). *Diagnostic and statistical manual of mental disorders* (4th ed.). Washington, DC: Author.

American Psychiatric Association. (1987). *Diagnostic and statistical manual of mental disorders* (3rd ed., revised). Washington, DC: Author.

American Psychiatric Association. (1994b). Practice guideline for the treatment of patients with bipolar disorder. *American Journal of Psychiatry, 151* (Suppl.).

American Psychiatric Association. (1995*). Diagnostic and statistical manual of mental disorders (4th ed.), Primary care version.* Washington, DC: Author.

Baldessarini, R. J. & Tarazi, F. I. (2001). Drugs and the treatment of psychiatric disorders: Psychosis and mania. In J. G. Hardman, L. E. Limbird, & A. G. Gilman (Eds.), *Goodman and Gilman's The pharmacological basis of therapeutics, 10th edition* (pp.485-520). New York, NY: McGraw-Hill.

Barloon, T. J. & Noyes, R. (1997). Charles Darwin and panic disorder. *Journal of the American Medical Association, 277,* 138-141.

Barnes, T. R. E. (1989). A rating scale for drug-induced akathisia. *British Journal of Psychiatry, 154,* 672-676.

Barnes, T. R. E. (1992). Neuromuscular effects of neuroleptics: Akathisia. In J. M. Kane & J. A. Lieberman (Eds.), *Adverse effects of psychotropic drugs.* New York, NY: Guilford Press.

Baumeister, A. A., Sevin, J. A., & King, B. H. (1998). Neuroleptics. In S. Reiss & M. G. Aman (Eds.), *Psychotropic medications and developmental disabilities: The International Consensus handbook* (pp. 133-150). Columbus, OH: O.S.U. Nisonger Center.

Bihm, E. M., Litton, F., & Poindexter, A. R. (1996). Functional analysis and treatment of severe behavior problems. In A. F. Rotatori, J. O. Schwenn, & S. Burkhardt (Eds.) *Advances in special education: Assessment and psychopathology issues in special education.* Greenwich, CT: JAI Press.

Broadhead, W. E., Blazer, D. G., George, L. K., & Tse, C. K. (1990). Depression, disability days, and days lost from work in a prospective epidemiologic survey. *Journal of the American Medical Association, 264,* 2524-2528.

Calvocoressi, L., Libman, D., Vegso, S. J., McDouble, C. J., & Price, L. H. (1998). Global functioning of inpatients with obsessive-compulsive disorder, schizophrenia, and major depression. *Psychiatric Services, 49,* 379-381.

Campbell, M. & Malone, R. P. (1991). Mental retardation and psychiatric disorders. *Hospital and Community Psychiatry, 42,* 374-379.

Charlot, L. R. (1997). Irritability, aggression, and depression in adults with mental retardation: A developmental perspective. *Psychiatric Annals, 27,* 190-197.

Council on Scientific Affairs, American Medical Association. (1993). The etiologic features of depression in adults. *Archives of Family Medicine, 2,* 76-84.

Crews, W. D., Bonaventura, S., Hay, C. L., Steele, W. K., & Rowe, F. B. (1993). Gilles de la Tourette disorder among individuals with severe or profound mental retardation. *Mental Retardation, 31,* 25-28.

Cross-National Collaborative Group. (1992). The changing rate of major depression: Cross-national comparisons. *Journal of the American Medical Association, 268,* 3098-3105.

Cummings, J. L. (1993, May 30). The mental status examination. *Hospital Practice,* pp. 56-68.

Desrochers, M. N., Hile, M. G., & Williams-Moseley, T. L. (1997). Survey of functional assessment procedures used with individuals who display mental retardation and severe problem behaviors. *American Journal on Mental Retardation, 101,* 535-546.

DiBartolomeo, A. & Kaniecki, J. (1996, May). *Survey for depression in an institutionalized population.* Paper presented at the meeting of the American Association on Mental Retardation, San Antonio, TX.

Elliott, F. A. (1984). The episodic dyscontrol syndrome and aggression. *Neurologic Clinics, 2,* 113-125.

El-Mallakh, R. S., Wright, J. C., Breen, K. J., & Lippmann, S. B. (1996). Clues to depression in primary care practice. *Postgraduate Medicine, 100,* 85-96.

Feifel, D. (1996). Attention-deficit hyperactivity disorder in adults. *Postgraduate Medicine, 100,* 207-216.

Ferris, F. O. (1995). Depression in the medically ill patient. In R. J. Cadieux (Ed.), *Depression in the primary care patient.* Minneapolis, MN: McGraw-Hill.

Fletcher, R. J. & Poindexter, A. R. (1996, Jan./Feb./Mar.). Current trends in mental health care for persons with mental retardation. *Journal of Rehabilitation.* 22-25.

Frances, A. & First, M. B. (1998). *Your mental health: A layman's guide to the psychiatrist's Bible.* New York: Scribner.

Gable, R. A. (1996). A critical analysis of functional assessment: Issues for researchers and practitioners. *Behavioral Disorders, 22,* 36-40.

Gedye, A. (1996). Issues involved in recognizing obsessive-compulsive disorder in developmentally disabled clients. *Seminars in Clinical Neuropsychiatry, 1,* 142-147.

Gualtieri, C. T., Quade, D., Hicks, R. E., Mayo, J. P., & Schroeder, S. R. (1984). Tardive dyskinesia and other clinical consequences of neuroleptic treatment in children and adolescents. *American Journal of Psychiatry, 141,* 20-23.

Hanzel, T. I., Kalachnik, J. E., & Harder, S. R. (1992). A case of phenobarbital exacerbation of a preexisting maladaptive behavior partially suppressed by chlorpromazine and misinterpreted as chlorpromazine efficacy. *Research in Developmental Disabilities, 13,* 381-392.

Health Care Financing Administration, Health Standards and Quality Bureau, Center for Long Term Care (1996). *Psychopharmacological medications: Safety precautions for persons with developmental disabilities.* Baltimore, MD: Author.

Hill, J. C. & Schoener, E. P. (1996). Age-dependent decline of attention deficit hyperactivity disorder. *American Journal of Psychiatry, 153,* 1143-1146.

Hollifield, M., Katon, W., Skipper, B., Chapman, T., Ballenger, J. C., Mannuzza, S., & Fyer, A. J. (1997). Panic disorder and quality of life: Variables predictive of functional impairment. *American Journal of Psychiatry, 154,* 766-772.

Holt, G. (1998). Diagnostic dilemmas: The diagnosis of mental illness in people with mental retardation. *The NADD Bulletin, 1,* 66-68.

Hudson, J. I., Lipinski, J. F., Frankenburg, F. R., Grochocinski, V. J., & Kupfer, D. J. (1988). Electroencephalographic sleep in mania. *Archives of General Psychiatry, 45,* 267-273.

Hurley, A. D. & Sovner, R. (1988). The clinical characteristics and management of borderline personality disorder in mentally retarded persons, *Psychiatric Aspects of Mental Retardation Reviews, 7,* 43-51.

Hurley, A. D. & Sovner, R. (1992). Inventories for evaluating psychopathology in developmentally diabled individuals. *The Habilitative Mental Healthcare Newsletter, 11,* 45-50.

Hyde, T. M. & Weinberger, D. R. (1995). Tourette's syndrome: A model neuropsychiatric disorder. *Journal of the American Medical Association, 273,* 498-501.

Jenkins, H. W. (1996, October 8). The latest management craze: Crazy management. *The Wall Street Journal*, p. A23.

Katerndahl, D. A. & Realini, J. P. (1995). Where do panic attack sufferers seek care?. *Journal of Family Practice, 40,* 237-243.

Katerndahl, D. A. & Trammell, C. (1997). Prevalence and recognition of panic states in STARNET patients presenting with chest pain. *Journal of Family Practice, 45,* 54-63.

Kerbeshian, J., Burd, L., & Klug, M. G. (1995). Comorbid Tourette's disorder and bipolar disorder: An etiologic perspective. *American Journal of Psychiatry, 152,* 1646-1651.

King, B. H., DeAntonio, C., McCracken, J. T., Forness, S. R., & Ackerland, V. (1994). Psychiatric consultation in severe and profound mental retardation. *American Journal of Psychiatry, 151,* 1802-1808.

Klein, D. N., Ouimette, P. C., Kelly, H. S., Ferro, T., & Riso, L. P. (1994). Test-retest reliability of team consensus best-estimate diagnoses of axis I and II disorders in a family study. *American Journal of Psychiatry, 151,*1043-1047.

Klerman, G. L. & Weissman, M. M. (1989). Increasing rates of depression. *Journal of the American Medical Association, 261,* 2229-2235.

Khreim, I. & Mikkelsen, E. (1996). Panic disorder in the developmentally disabled adult. In R. Friedlander & D. Sobsey (Eds.). *13th Annual Conference Proceedings: Through the Lifespan* (pp. 189-190). Kingston, NY: NADD Press.

Khreim, I. & Mikkelsen, E. (1997). Anxiety disorders in adults with mental retardation. *Psychiatric Annals, 27,* 175-181.

Kuhlman, T. L., Sincaban, V. A., & Bernstein, M. J. (1990). Team use of the Global Assessment Scale for inpatient planning and evaluation. *Hospital and Community Psychiatry, 41,* 416-419.

Lamb, H. R. (1997). The denial of severe mental illness. *Psychiatric Services, 48,* 1367.

Leaman, T. L. (1993). Anxiety disorders: Reaching the untreated. *The Female Patient, 18,* 99-102.

Lebowitz, B. D., Pearson, J. L., Schneider, L. S., Reynolds, C. F., Alexopoulos, G. S., Bruce, M. L., Conwell, Y., Katz, I. R., Meyers, B. S., Morrison, M. F., Mossey, J., Niederehe, G., & Parmelee, P. (1997). Diagnosis and treatment of depression in late life: Consensus statement update. *Journal of the American Medical Association, 278,* 1186-1190.

Lewine, J. D., Andrews, R., Chez, M., Patil, A. A., Devinsky, O., Smith, M., Kanner, A., Davis, J. T., Funke, M., Jones, G., Chong, B., Provencal, S., Weisend, M., Lee, R. R., & Orrison, W. W. (1999). Magnetoencephalographic patterns of epileptiform activity in children with regressive autism spectrum disorders. *Pediatrics, 104,* 405-418.

Loschen, E. L. & Saliga, C. A. (2000). Anxiety disorders in a clinic population. In A. R. Poindexter (Ed.), *Assessment and treatment of anxiety disorders in persons with mental retardation.* Kingston, NY: NADD Press

Lowry, M. A. (1993). When functional analysis of problem behavior and desired treatment outcomes are not enough. *The Habilitative Mental Healthcare Newsletter, 12,* 87-90.

Lowry, M. A. (1995). Anger: A root of problem behaviors in the depressed. *The Habilitative Mental Healthcare Newsletter, 14,* 101-106.

Malloy, E., Zealberg, J. J., & Paolone, T. (1998). A patient with mental retardation and possible panic disorder. *Psychiatric Services, 49,* 105-106.

Marston, G. M., Perry, D. W., & Roy, A. (1997). Manifestations of depression in people with intellectual disability. *Journal of Intellectual Disability Research, 41,* 476-480.

Matson, J. L. (1983). Depression in the mentally retarded: Toward a conceptual analysis of diagnosis. *Progress in Behavior Modification, 15,* 57-79.

McGlynn, T. J. & Metcalf, H. L. (Eds.) (1989). *Diagnosis and treatment of anxiety disorders: A physician's handbook.* Washington, DC: American Psychiatric Press.

Menolascino, F. & Fleischer, M. (1993). Mental health care in the mentally retarded: Past, present, and future. In R. Fletcher & A. Dosen (Eds.*), Mental health aspects of mental retardation: Progress in assessment and treatment* (pp.18-41). Lexington, MA: Lexington Books.

Miller, M. W. (1994, Jan. 14). Survey sketches new portrait of the mentally ill. *Wall Street Journal*, p. B1.

Moss, S., Prosser, H., Ibbotson, B., & Goldberg, D. (1996). Respondent and informant accounts of psychiatric symptoms in a sample of patients with learning disability. *Journal of Intellectual Disability Research,* 40, 457-465.

Neville, B. G. R. (1999). Magnetoencephalographic patterns of epileptiform activity in children with regressive autism spectrum disorders (commentary). *Pediatrics, 103,* 558.

Nies, A. S. & Spielberg, S. P. (2001). Principles of therapeutics. In J. G. Hardman, L. E. Limbird, & A. G. Gilman (Eds.), *Goodman and Gilman's The pharmacological basis of therapeutics, 10th edition* (pp.45-66). New York, NY: McGraw-Hill.

Papolos, D. F., Faedda, G. L., Veit, S., Goldberg, R., Morrow, B., Kucherlapati, R., & Shprintzen, R. J. (1996). Bipolar spectrum disorders in patients diagnosed with velo-cardio-facial syndrome: Does a hemizygous deletion of chromosome 22q11 result in bipolar affective disorder? *American Journal of Psychiatry, 153,* 1541-1547.

Pary, R. J. (1997). What is the short-term effect of depression on adaptive behavior? *The Habilitative Mental Healthcare Newsletter, 16,* 48-49.

Patients can confuse the similar symptoms of asthma and panic. (1997, August). *Modern Medicine, 65,* 43.

Plumlee, A. A. (1986). Biologic rhythms and affective illness. *Journal of Psychosocial Nursing, 24,* 12-17.

Poindexter, A. R. (1994). Weight changes with neuroleptic withdrawal. *NADD Newsletter, 11,* 7-8.

Poindexter, A. R. & Bihm, E. M. (1994). Incidence of short-sleep patterns in institutionalized individuals with profound mental retardation. *American Journal on Mental Retardation, 98,* 776-780.

Poindexter, A. R., Berglund, J. A., & Kolstoe, P. D. (1993). Changes in antiepileptic drug prescribing patterns in large institutions: Preliminary results of a five-year experience. *American Journal on Mental Retardation, 98* (Suppl.), 34-40.

Poindexter, A. R., Bihm, E. M., & Litton, F. W. (1996). Dual diagnosis and severe behavior problems. In A. F. Rotatori, J. O. Schwenn, & S. Burkhardt (Eds.) *Advances in special education: Assessment and psychopathology issues in special education.* Greenwich, CT: JAI Press.

Pyles, D. A. M., Muniz, K., Cade, A., & Silva, R. (1997). A behavioral diagnostic paradigm for integrating behavior-analytic and psychopharmacological interventions for people with a dual diagnosis. *Research in Developmental Disabilities, 18,* 185-214.

Pyne, J. M., Patterson, T. L., Kaplan, R. M., Gillin, J. C., Koch, W. L., & Grant, I. (1997). Assessment of the quality of life of patients with major depression. *Psychiatric Services, 48,* 224-230.

Reiss, S. (1994). *Handbook of challenging behavior: Mental health aspects of mental retardation.* Huntington, OH: IDS Publishing.

Roberts, R. E., Kaplan, G. A., Shema, S. J., & Strawbridge, W. J. (1997). Does growing old increase the risk for depression? *American Journal of Psychiatry, 154,* 1384-1390.

Rosenbaum, J. F. (1996, August). Panic disorder in the emergency department. *Emergency Medicine,* p. 54-69.

Rosenquist, P. B. (2000). Tourette's syndrome and obsessive compulsive disorder: Treatable causes of complex repetitive movements in mental retardation/developmental disability. In A. R. Poindexter (Ed.), *Assessment and treatment of anxiety disorders in persons with mental retardation.* Kingston, NY: NADD Press.

Rosenquist, P. B. & Bodfish, J. W. (1997). Neuropsychiatric movement disorders in those with mental retardation or developmental disability. *Psychiatric Annals, 27,* 213-218.

Rowe, M. G., Fleming, M. F., Barry, K. L., Manwell, L. B., & Kropp, S. (1995). Correlates of depression in primary care. *The Journal of Family Practice, 41,* 551-558.

Ryan, R. (2000). Post-traumatic stress disorder in persons with developmental disabilities. In A. R. Poindexter (Ed.), *Assessment and treatment of anxiety disorders in persons with mental retardation.* Kingston, NY: N.A.D.D.

Samuels, J. F., Nestadt, G., Romanoski, A. J., Folstein, M. F., & McHugh, P. R. (1994). DSM-III personality disorders in the community. *American Journal of Psychiatry, 151,* 1055-1062.

Schmaling, K. B. & Bell, J. (1997). Asthma and panic disorder. *Archives of Family Medicine, 6,* 20-23.

Shaffer, D. (1994). Attention deficit hyperactivity disorder in adults. *American Journal of Psychiatry, 151,* 633-638.

Shea, M. T. (1995). Interrelationships among categories of personality disorders. In W. J. Livesley (Ed.), *The DSM-IV personality disorders.* New York: Guilford Press.

Silka, V. R. & Hauser, M. J. (1997). Psychiatric assessment of the person with mental retardation. *Psychiatric Annals, 27,* 162-169.

Snaith, R. P. (1993, September 30). Identifying depression: The significance of anhedonia. *Hospital Practice,* 55-60.

Sovner, R. (1990, December*). Differential diagnosis of violence.* Paper presented at the meeting of the National Association for the Dually Diagnosed (Mental Health and Mental Retardation), Boston, MA.

Sovner, R. (1996). Six models of behavior from a neuropsychiatric perspective. *The Habilitative Mental Healthcare Newsletter, 15,* 51-54.

Sovner, R. & Hurley, A. D. (1982a). Hydrocephalus and the cocktail party syndrome. *Psychiatric Aspects of Mental Retardation Newsletter, 1,* 13-16.

Sovner, R. & Hurley, A. D. (1982b). Diagnosing mania in the mentally retarded. *Psychiatric Aspects of Mental Retardation Newsletter, l,* 9-11.

Sovner, R. & Hurley, A. D. (1983a). Preparing for a mental health consultation. *Psychiatric Aspects of Mental Retardation Newsletter, 2,* 37-40.

Sovner, R. & Hurley, A. D. (1983b). The mental status examination. *Psychiatric Aspects of Mental Retardation Newsletter, 2,* 5-12.

Sovner, R. & Hurley, A. D. (1986). Four factors affecting the diagnosis of psychiatric disorders in mentally retarded persons. *Psychiatric Aspects of Mental Retardation Newsletter, 5,* 45-50.

Sovner, R., Hurley, A. D., & LaBrie, R. A. (1982). Diagnosing depression in the mentally retarded. *Psychiatric Aspects of Mental Retardation Newsletter, 1,* 1-4.

Sung, H., Hawkinds, B. A., Eklund, S. J., Kim, K. A., Foose, A., May, M. E., & Rogers, N. B. (1997). Depression and dementia in aging adults with Down syndrome: A case study approach. *Mental Retardation, 35,* 27-38.

Szymanski, L. S., King, B., Goldberg, B., Reid, A. H., Tonge, B. J., & Cain, N. (1998). Diagnosis of mental disorders in people with mental retardation. In S. Reiss & M. G. Aman (Eds.), *Psychotropic medications and developmental disabilities: The International Consensus handbook* (pp. 3-17). Columbus, OH: O.S.U. Nisonger Center.

Taylor, M. A. (1997, February 15). Evaluation and management of attention-deficit hyperactivity disorder, *American Family Physician,* 887-897.

Torrey, W. C. (1993). Psychiatric care of adults with developmental disabilities and mental illness in the community. *Community Mental Health Journal, 29,* 461-476.

Vining, E. P. G., Mellits, E. D., Dorsen, M. M., Cataldo, M. F., Quaskey, S. A., Spielberg, S. P., & Freeman, J. M. (1987). Psychologic and behavioral effects of antiepileptic drugs in children: A double-blind comparison between phenobarbital and valproic acid. *Pediatrics, 80,* 165-174.

Vitiello, B. & Behar, D. (1992). Mental retardation and psychiatric illness. *Hospital and Community Psychiatry, 43,* 494-499.

Volavka, J. (1995). *Neurobiology of violence.* Washington, DC: American Psychiatric Press.

Werry, J. S. (1998). Anxiolytics and sedatives. In S. Reiss & M. G. Aman (Eds.), *Psychotropic medications and developmental disabilities: The International Consensus handbook* (pp. 201-214). Columbus, OH: O.S.U. Nisonger Center.

Widiger, T. A. & Frances, A. J. (1988). Personality disorders. In J. A. Talbott, R. E. Hales, & S. C. Yudofsky (Eds.), *Textbook of psychiatry*. Washington, DC: American Psychiatric Press.

Wood, A. J. J. (1994). Adverse reactions to drugs. In K. J. Isselbacher, E. Braunwald, J. D. Wilson, J. B. Martin, A. S. Fauci, & D. L. Kasper (Eds.), *Harrison's Principles of internal medicine* (pp. 405-412). New York, NY: McGraw-Hill.

Zoler, M. L. (1995, July 15). One-third of women develop anxiety disorders. *Family Practice News,* p. 30.

Zung, W. W. K., Broadhead, W. E., & Roth, M. E. (1993). Prevalence of depressive symptoms in primary care. *The Journal of Family Practice, 37,* 337-344.

INTRODUCTION TO DUAL DIAGNOSIS (MENTAL HEALTH/BEHAVIORAL DISORDERS IN PERSON WITH MENTAL RETARDATION)

Instructions for use of this self-directed instruction program:

- Cover the right-hand side of each page, since this gives the answer to the questions.
- Read each section carefully, and WRITE your answer in the designated place.
- After WRITING your answer, check and see if you are correct.
- Refer to your handout materials as necessary.

INTRODUCTION TO DUAL DIAGNOSIS (MENTAL HEALTH/BEHAVIORAL DISORDERS IN PERSON WITH MENTAL RETARDATION)

A very important and exciting current area of interest for people working with persons with developmental disabilities is that of "dual diagnosis"—diagnosis and treatment of psychopathologic problems in persons with mental retardation. People with mental retardation can, indeed, have any mental health problems that anyone else has—but diagnosis may be more difficult (but not impossible). "Dual diagnosis" means the person has mental retardation and m________________ health problems.

mental (Another definition for dual diagnosis, not implied in these materials, is substance abuse and some other psychiatric condition.)

Accuracy of diagnosis is extremely important in development of really good treatment programs. Recent emphasis on an interdisciplinary team approach to care for persons with mental retardation has put in place an important information gathering source to facilitate diagnosis and assessment of psychiatric problems in these folks. The interdisciplinary team is (of vital importance or somewhat important?) in assessment of people with possible dual diagnosis.

____

of vital importance!!

A number of pieces of information need to be in place before any mental consultation for anyone, but particularly for those persons who may have problems giving a history themselves. Important information includes 1) the reason for referral; 2) duration of problem; and 3) presence of precipitators (what makes the problem worse). Significant emotional and/

or physical events which directly precede the onset of behavior problems should be assessed as p____________________.

precipitators (These might possibly include day of week, time of day, persons present, site, etc..)

Information should be furnished to the clinician related to 4) mental retardation level, and 5) psychosocial status. Psychosocial status information should include current living and social arrangements and education, vocation, and recreational programs in which the person participates. In 6), names of primary contact persons should be included. Consultants should be furnished (extensive information or only "vital" facts?) about the referred individual.

____

extensive information (well-organized, of course, for ease of retrieval of information)

7), All present medical diagnoses should be carefully listed, with names of physicians/clinics where the person is being treated. Causes of mental retardation should be included. Every medication and/or treatment the person is receiving should be listed, including "over the counter," nutritional supplements, and herbal or other "natural" products. Information should include dosage levels, schedules, and prescribing physician. (All or Only psychotropic?) medication information is of importance. ____________________

All (Many medications used for general medical conditions have behavioral or psychotropic side effects.)

8), All previous mental health interventions should be outlined, with dates of treatment, type problem, and name of treating clinician/mental health agency. (Past history for as far back as can possibly be obtained may be of vital importance in both development of a rational diagnosis and an effective treatment program.) True or false?: Drug treatment history for five years is enough to keep in current files. ________________

false (Drug history back 30 years [or more] may be very important. Summary of this information should be maintained on current chart indefinitely.)

9), Any family history of mental illness should be carefully noted, since many mental health conditions seem to "run" in families. For each family member with history of mental illness, the type of problem, treatment dates, and information about treating clinicians/agencies should be included, if available. True or false?: Every mental health condition seems to be primarily of environmental rather than genetic origin. ______________

false (While many mental health conditions seem to result at least in part from environmental conditions, familial and/or genetic factors are still very important.)

10), Extensive information about vegetative functioning and behavior should be listed for the clinician: energy level, appetite, weight change, sleep pattern, and presence of fecal/urinary incontinence (if a new behavior). Appetite may be followed most easily by weight changes. Changes in sleep pattern, energy level, and appetite are examples of v____________ changes.

vegetative

Most mental health professionals do some sort of mental status assessment when assessing anyone, whether or not that person has mental retardation. (This assessment is often informal, but it does occur.) A mental status examination includes assessment of general behavior and appearance, with observation of activity and purposefulness. An individual's activity may be under(hypo-)active or h_________________.

hyperactive

While a person's activity may be either hyperactive or underactive, it also may be purposeful or may appear to occur entirely at random. They may also appear agitated, or far too quiet. Another part of observing a person's general behavior and appearance is how he/she contacts the environment—is the person cooperative? Can he/she follow instructions? Do they make eye contact? True or false?: an individual should be studied in isolation from the environment. ________________

false

Other behavioral observations include facial expressions, including whether or not there is a full range of expressions, and whether those expressions seem appropriate to the situation. Unusual behaviors and postures are carefully observed, including mannerisms, rituals, stereotyped behaviors, self-injurious behavior, and abnormal posturing. Facial expressions of people with mental retardation are (significant or usually only silly?). ____________________

significant

Speech and thought processes are also analyzed during a mental status examination. In assessment of speech productivity, note is made about whether or not the person speaks spontaneously, and whether or not his/her speech imitates others or repeats the same thing over and over (perseveration). Also, speech rate may be increased, decreased, or essentially normal. The technical word for repeating words over and over is p________________.

perseveration

Some degree of assessment of speech organization is also made—whether ideas seem appropriate, fanciful, etc.. Content of speech should also be assessed: is the speech goal-directed? Are there any recurrent themes? What is the tone of each theme—sad, elated, angry, grandiose? Grandiosity is an example of a tone of speech t______________.

theme

Mood and affect are carefully analyzed during a mental status examination. Range of emotional expression is assessed—broad, expansive, restrictive, blunted? Note is made about appropriateness of expressions of emotions to speech content and to external events, and whether or not there is mood lability (lots of ups and downs), and whether or not the mood seems pervasive. An individual with many mood swings is said to have mood ________________.	lability
Presence or absence of psychotic symptoms is determined. If a person is seeing, hearing, smelling, tasting, or touching something which is not there, he/she is said to be hallucinating. If a person strongly believes something which obviously is not true, he/she is said to have a delusion. The technical word for a false sensory perception is h____________________.	hallucination
Other psychiatric symptoms, such as phobias (fears), compulsive behaviors, and obsessional thoughts are also assessed. When a person has particular fears, he/she is apt to avoid the feared object(s). The technical term for a specific fear is ____________________.	phobia
A complete mental status examination also includes some assessment of cognitive (thought) function. This may include whether or not the person knows who he/she is, where he/she is, the day, the date, etc.. Other aspects of cognitive assessment might include whether or not the person is paying attention and how good their memory is. Orientation to time and place is part of c________________ (thought) assessment.	cognitive

The process of making a psychiatric diagnosis in a person with mental retardation is influenced by four non-specific factors associated with mental retardation. First, *intellectual distortion*, defined as effects of concrete thinking and impaired communication skills, often results in the inability of the person to label his/her own experiences, and to describe those experiences. True or false?: A person with mental retardation usually can state clearly how he/she feels and what his/her mood is. ______________

false (We should, however, ask them about their experiences and feelings. Sometimes they don't tell us because we don't ask!!

The second non-specific factor is *psychosocial*, defined as the effect(s) of impoverished social skills and life experiences. This may result clinically in an unsophisticated presentation and lack of poise during the interview with a clinician. This can result in either over- or under-diagnosis of psychiatric conditions. Psychiatric symptoms may be (missed, over-diagnosed, or both missed and over-diagnosed?) in persons with mental retardation.

____

both missed and overdiagnosed (Nervousness and silliness may be misdiagnosed as psychiatric features, or symptoms may be completely missed.)

A third factor is *cognitive disintegration*, where because of stress information processing is disrupted. A person with mental retardation who is stressed may look quite bizarre and even psychotic, and may be misdiagnosed as having schizophrenia. (This may result in inappropriate drug treatment.) Bizarre symptoms in a person with mental retardation may be a result of s______________ rather than a psychiatric disorder.

stress

A fourth non-specific factor that may influence the process of making a psychiatric diagnosis is *baseline exaggeration,* which is an increase in severity of pre-existing cognitive deficits and maladaptive behaviors due to a psychiatric disorder. This causes problems in establishing illness features, target symptoms, and outcome measures. A person with a long history of SIB (self-injurious behavior) may have an increase in symptoms when he/she becomes depressed, due to b________________ e__________________.

baseline exaggeration (They may also test at a lower cognitive level when they become depressed or develop some other psychiatric disorder.)

PART 2

The American Psychiatric Association published a fourth edition of its *Diagnostic and Statistical Manual of Mental Disorders*, better known as "DSM-IV," in 1994, to assist with classification of mental disorders. The common name for the fourth edition of APA's classification manual is ________________.

DSM-IV ("dee ess emm four")

The DSM-IV clearly states that the mental disorders it describes represent clinically significant behavioral or psychological patterns that occur in a person, and that are associated with present distress or disability in that person, or with a significantly increased risk of suffering death, pain, disability, or an important loss of freedom. Behavior that is only inconvenient for others (is or isn't?) considered as a disorder in DSM-IV. ________________

isn't (Neither deviant behavior nor conflicts primarily between the person and society are mental disorders unless they cause distress as noted above.)

"A common misconception is that a classification of mental disorders classifies people, when actually what re being classified are disorders that people have." For this reason the text of DSM-IV avoids the use of such expressions as "a schizophrenic," but uses terms as "a person with schizophrenia." The DSM-IV (does or doesn't?) use "people first" language. ________________

does (as should we all!)

The DSM-IV does not assume that each category of mental disorder has distinct boundaries, but acknowledges the overlapping of many disorders. It also does not assume that all people with the same mental disorder are alike in all ways, or will respond to treatment in exactly the same ways. Most people with a given mental disorder such as depression are (alike or different in many ways?).

____

different in many ways (while sharing many common symptoms)

The DSM-IV is based on a *multiaxial system*, which involves assessment on five axes, each of which refers to a different "domain" of information. Axis I includes clinical disorders and other conditions that may be a focus of clinical attention. Axis II includes mental retardation and personality disorders, and Axis III lists general medical conditions. While mental retardation is on Axis II, epilepsy is on Axis _________.

III (since it is a general medical condition)

According to the DSM-IV multiaxial system, Axis IV includes psychosocial and environmental problems that may affect the diagnosis, treatment, and general outcome of mental disorders. Axis V, Global Assessment of Functioning (GAF), is for reporting the clinician's judgement of the person's overall level of functioning. Homelessness or a recent divorce are examples of p________________ problems, which should be listed on Axis IV.

psychosocial

Major groups of Axis I disorders include disorders usually first diagnosed in infancy, childhood, or adolescence (except mental retardation); delirium, dementia, and amnestic and other cognitive disorders; mental disorders due to a general medical condition (formerly called "organic"); and substance-related disorders. Mental disorders due to a general medical condition were formerly called ________________.

organic

Present DSM-IV name for the condition formerly called "Organic Mood Disorder" is ________________________________.

Mood Disorder due to General Medical Condition

Other major groups of Axis I disorders include schizophrenia and other psychotic disorders; mood disorders; anxiety disorders; somatoform disorders; factitious disorders; dissociative disorders; and sexual and gender identity disorders. "Multiple Personality Disorder" is now referred to as Dissociative Identity Disorder, and is included in Axis __________.

I

Additional major groups of Axis I disorders include eating disorders, sleep disorders, impulse-control disorders not otherwise specified, adjustment disorders, and other conditions that may be a focus of clinical attention. Other conditions that may be a focus of clinical attention are often described as "V-code" conditions. Mental/behavioral conditions not otherwise described in DSM-IV that receive clinical attention are called ____________ conditions.

V-code

In an oral presentation at a national NADD meeting in Boston in 1990, Dr. Robert Sovner listed five causes of psychopathology in persons with mental retardation: 1) learned maladaptive behavior; 2) central nervous system dysfunction; 3) childhood onset pervasive developmental disorder (which includes autism); 4) classic psychiatric disorders; and 5) medical/drug-induced disorders. True or false?: Autism is a pervasive developmental disorder. ________

True

Dr. Sovner's "differential diagnosis" list can be very useful as interdisciplinary team members attempt to work out possible causes of difficult behavior problems and attempt to develop rational treatment programs. Each of his five categories fits in in some way into the DSM-IV system. Often people with difficult problems exhibit more than one of these causes—even all five in the same person. True or false?: Self-injurious behavior may be due to more than one cause. ___________

True (A particular "behavior" may be due to any or all of the five categories.)

Drug treatment is not necessarily required for conditions in any of the five categories, but may be helpful in some. True or false?: Drug treatment is always required for a person with a classical psychiatric condition. ___________

false (Drug treatment is often helpful for some classical psychiatric disorders, however.)

Many people with mental retardation have behavioral difficulties at least partly due to Sovner's first category, learned maladaptive behavior. Many of these individuals have lived in places for long periods of time where they have watched and copied all sorts of unpleasant behaviors, or where various "bad" behaviors were reinforced for one reason or another. Learned maladaptive behavior is (rare or common?) in people who lived for many years in institutions. ______________

common

True or false?: Learned maladaptive behavior almost never occurs when people have lived all their lives in their family homes. ____________

false (Behavior can be reinforced as readily at home as anywhere else.)

As an example of learned maladaptive behavior, an individual may have begun banging his ears when he developed an ear-ache, but then may have found this an effective way to avoid situations he perceives as not desirable—if he bangs his ears he may not be required to go to work or to take a bath. If a person is not required to do something unpleasant to him when he engages in self-injurious behavior, the effectiveness of that behavior is being r__________________.

reinforced

In general, learned maladaptive behavior is not particularly responsive to medication treatment. Since these behaviors may have persisted for many years, successful treatment programs often require a combination of behavioral therapy and environmental management, plus a lot of patience and a lot of time. Treatment programs for learned maladaptive behavior are (usually quick or often length?) in duration before success is achieved. ____________________

often lengthy

Sovner's second category, central nervous system dysfunction, is often seen in persons with mental retardation, primarily because of their high frequency of brain damage. (Neurologists consider this category "episodic dyscontrol syndrome.") This condition is marked by recurrent attacks of uncontrollable rage, usually with very little provocation and often completely out of character. Persons with this condition (are calm or seem to have a "short fuse?") ______________________

seem to have a "short fuse"

People with episodic dyscontrol syndrome often have a psychiatric diagnosis of Personality Change due to General Medical Condition (formerly called Organic Personality Disorder) or Intermittent Explosive Disorder. Common DSM-IV diagnoses made in persons with central nervous system dysfunction are ____________________ ________ and ______________________________.

Personality Change due to General Medical Condition or Intermittent Explosive Disorder

Sometimes people with dyscontrol problems benefit from medication treatment, but many are treated successfully with behavior management and various kinds of group therapy, without drugs. Various types of "anger management" approaches which teach individuals ways of controlling impulses themselves, offer encouraging results. True or false?: Everyone with intermittent explosive disorder must be treated with psychotropic medication.

____

false

One type Personality Change due to General Medical Condition which is not specifically discussed in DSM-IV is *Cocktail Party Syndrome,* a neuropsychological condition associated with hydrocephalus. People with this condition often are "chatty," with speech of very superficial content. They have unstable emotions, poor judgement, and may appear to be maladjusted. Persons with cocktail party syndrome may appear (boring or witty but superficial?).

____

witty but superficial

People with cocktail party syndrome often have cognitive levels in the range of mental retardation, but there is significant difference between verbal IQ and performance IQ. They also have visual-perceptual defects. Persons

with cocktail party syndrome usually have verbal IQs (higher or lower?) than performance IQ levels. ________________	higher
Experts note the importance of families and staff working with individuals with cocktail party syndrome having a realistic sense of that person's abilities, since pressure from others may cause the affected individual to blame himself/herself for failing to live up to expectations. True or false?: Persons with cocktail party syndrome can function much higher than they usually do if they really try. ______________	false (Anxiety and/or depression may result if unrealistic goals have been set for the individual.)
One condition that may be considered under central nervous system disorder is Tourette Disorder (and other tic disorders). Tics are sudden, rapid, recurrent, nonrhythmic stereotyped motor movements or vocalizations. Persons with Tourette Disorder have both multiple vocal and multiple motor tics, usually in "spells" or bouts, many times per day. Onset is before age 18. Tourette disorder is a t______ disorder.	tic
While Attention-Deficit/Hyperactivity Disorder (ADHD) was thought in the past to only occur in children, recent studies indicate that it often persists into adult life. Persons with this condition may have either inattention or hyperactivity-impulsivity. Persons with inattention often fail to notice details and make many careless mistakes. They don't seem to listen when others speak to them. True or false?: Only children and teenagers have ADHD. ______________	false

Persons with ADHD and inattention often fail to follow through on instructions and fail to finish tasks. They seem to have trouble organizing tasks and activities, and may not want to engage in things that require sustained mental effort, such as schoolwork or homework. They may lose things necessary for the jobs they are supposed to be doing. Persons with ADHD are (usually dependable or often considered undependable?) in everyday life. ____________________

often considered undependable

Persons with ADHD who are hyperactive-impulsive are often fidgety, and leave classroom seats and/or often run around when they are supposed to be quiet. They often talk a lot, and may blurt out answers to questions before the questions have been completed. They may seem impatient, and often interrupt or intrude on others. Persons with ADHD are (usually considered polite and well-mannered or often considered rude?). ____________________

often considered rude

PART 3

When a new behavior problem develops in a person who is receiving any kind of medication, particularly a new medication or a dosage increase of an old medication, some kind of drug reaction should be the first consideration. As an example, when neuroleptic ("major" tranquilizer) drugs are introduced, or dosages are increased, *akathisia* may develop. Akathisia is associated with treatment with n________________ drugs.

neuroleptic ("major") tranquilizer)

Akathisia is a term referring to strong subjective feelings of distress or discomfort, often referred to the legs, as well as to a compelling need to be in constant movement. A person receiving Haldol™ (a neuroleptic drug) who paces constantly and cannot seem to sit still may have a condition called a_________________.

akathisia

Akathisia can be mistaken for *agitation*. The distinction is very important, since agitation may be treated with an increase in drug dosage, and increased drug dosage may make akathisia worse. Because of this fact, akathisia symptoms (are or are not?) dose-related. ______________

are (the more drug, the worse the symptoms)

Treatment of akathisia typically requires reduction of neuroleptic drug dosage. Recent studies seem to indicate that there is a link between high doses of high-potency neuroleptics (such as Haldol™ and Prolixin™), akathisia, and violent behavior. Since people with developmental disabilities who are violent/aggressive are often given high-potency neuroleptic drugs in high dosages, they should be considered as at-risk for development of a_________________.

akathisia (which may make them more violent)

True or false?: Administration of high-potency neuroleptic drugs in high dosage often does not result in clear behavioral benefit. ____________

True

Neuroleptic-induced akathisia should be carefully looked for in any person being treated with high doses of high-potency neuroleptics, but particularly in those persons with a history of severe aggression. Fluphenazine (Prolixin™) is 85 times as strong as

Thorazine™. Haloperidol (Haldol™) is 62.5 times as strong as Thorazine™. Ten milligrams of Prolixin™ is equal to ______ mg chlorpromazine (Thorazine™).	850
Five mg Haldol™ four times a day is equivalent to ________ mg Thorazine™ per day.	1250
The technical term for a drug reaction resulting in strong subjective feelings of distress or discomfort, often referred to the legs, as well as to a powerful need to be in constant movement, is ____________________.	akathisia
When neuroleptic drug dosages are decreased, no matter how slowly, *neuroleptic withdrawal symptoms* and/or previously masked psychiatric illness may become evident. Some of these symptoms may be very severe in some people. Symptoms of *tardive dyskinesia*, a movement disorder, may develop when tranquilizers are tapered. This may be temporary, or symptoms may be persistent. True or false?: Symptoms of tardive dyskinesia always resolve when neuroleptics are discontinued. ____________	false
Other neuroleptic withdrawal symptoms may be nausea, vomiting, poor appetite, weight loss, and heavy sweating (diaphoresis). Weight loss may be quite severe and frightening, even in people who are quite slender before the taper is begun. Severe insomnia (sleeplessness) is another common symptom. Profound weight loss occurs with neuroleptic taper (only in relatively fat people or in people of all weight levels?). ____________________________________	in people of all weight levels (even with a very slow taper regimen)

Recent research suggests that people with decreased brain cortex tissue may be more apt to develop weight loss during taper of neuroleptic drugs. Some studies indicate that about ¾ of adults with mental retardation who have neuroleptic drug tapering will have significant weight loss. (Some of these people are obese to begin with, but others may be quite thin.) People with brain damage (may be or probably aren't?) more apt to lose weight during neuroleptic taper. ____________________

may be

True or false?: People undergoing tranquilizer tapering may have severe problems with insomnia. __________

True (even if insomnia was not a part of the symptoms for which the drug was originally prescribed)

The speed of neuroleptic taper probably has nothing to do with the occurrence of neuroleptic withdrawal symptoms. In most cases some critical dosage level seems to be crossed (downward) before symptoms begin to occur. True or false?: Fast neuroleptic tapers are probably more apt than slow tapers to result in neuroleptic withdrawal symptoms. ____________

false

When benzodiazepine drugs (such as Valium™, Ativan™, Restoril™, Klonopin™, and Tranxene™) are administered, some people have a marked disinhibiting reaction, which worsens with increased dosage—they may lose whatever inhibitions they may had previously. This is said to be rare, but probably is far more common in people with developmental disabilities than in the general population. Disinhibition (is or isn't?) at least partially a dose-related side effect. ______

is (the higher the dosage, the more severe the reaction)

Persons who have a disinhibiting reaction with one benzodiazepine drug probably will have problems with other drugs in the same category. An individual who gets really "silly" when receiving Ativan™ will probably (improve or have the same type?) reaction if switched to Klonopin™.

____

have the same type

True or false?: A person with sleep problems who appears to disinhibit when given Ativan™ for his/her anxiety will probably not respond well to Restoril™ for sleep. ______________

True (since Ativan™ and Restoril™ are both benzodiazepine drugs)

Some antiepileptic drugs have marked behavioral side effects, both in adults and children. Phenobarbital, Mysoline™, and other barbiturate anticonvulsant drugs may have marked unpleasant effects on behavior, particularly increased aggression, irritability, and refusal to cooperate. Since Mysoline™ is drug much like phenobarbital, it has (less than or the same?) behavioral side effects as phenobarbital. ______________

The same (so does Mebaral™)

Behavioral side effects of barbiturate drugs (only occur in children or occur in adults as well as children?)

____

occur in adults as well as children

While barbiturate drugs have been known for many years to cause hyperactivity in some children, they are also known depressants. True or false?: Phenobarbital may cause depression.

True

______________ THE END

INTRODUCTION TO DUAL DIAGNOSIS (MENTAL HEALTH/BEHAVIORAl DISORDERS IN PERSON WITH MENTAL RETARDATION)

Educational Objectives

Participants will be able to answer the following questions:

1. What are the general principles of assessment for psychiatric diagnosis in persons with developmental disabilities?
2. What information should be provided to the clinician to facilitate psychiatric diagnosis?
3. How can *Diagnostic and Statistical Manual of Mental Disorders* (4th edition) (DSM-IV) be used to facilitate psychiatric diagnosis in this population?
4. What role do learned maladaptive behavior and central nervous system dysfunction play in behavioral problems in persons with developmental disabilities?
5. What conditions are commonly misdiagnosed as psychopathology?

INTRODUCTION TO DUAL DIAGNOSIS (MENTAL HEALTH/BEHAVIORAL DISORDERS IN PERSON WITH MENTAL RETARDATION)

Pretest/Posttest

T F 1. The term dual diagnosis can have more than one meaning.

T F 2. Psychiatric diagnosis is usually readily established in per sons with mental retardation.

T F 3. Many medications used for general medical conditions have behavioral or psychotropic side effects.

T F 4. Drug treatment history should be maintained for a maxi mum of five years in current files.

T F 5. A mental status examination cannot be performed on any one with an IQ below 50.

T F 6. Perseveration mans repeating the same thing over and over.

T F 7. If a person sees, hears, smells, tastes, or touches something which is not there, he/she is said to be having a delusion.

T F 8. A person with mental retardation often has trouble stating clearly how he/she feels and what his/her mood is.

T F 9. Information processing usually is not affected by extreme stress.

T F 10. Behavior that is very inconvenient for others is considered a disorder in DSM-IV.

T F 11. The DSM-IV uses a multiaxial system for assessment.

T F 12. Organic Personality Disorder is a DSM-IV diagnosis.

T F 13. "Multiple Personality Disorder" is referred to as Dissociative Identity Disorder in DSM-IV.

T F 14. Self-injurious behavior may be due to more than one cause, in the same individual.

T F 15. Treatment programs for learned maladaptive behavior are often lengthy, before a successful outcome is achieved.

T F 16. Cocktail Party Syndrome is associated with microcephaly.

T F 17. Attention-Deficit/Hyperactivity Disorder only occurs in children.

T F 18. Akathisia may be mistaken for lethargy (excessive sleepiness).

T F 19. Prolixin™ is 85 times as strong as Thorazine™.

T F 20. Phenobarbital may cause both aggression and depression.

Name: ______________________

Position: ______________________

Date: ______________

INTRODUCTION TO DUAL DIAGNOSIS (MENTAL HEALTH/BEHAVIORALDISORDERS IN PERSON WITH MENTAL RETARDATION)

Answers to Pretest/Posttest

1. True
2. False
3. True
4. False
5. False
6. True
7. False
8. True
9. False
10. False
11. True
12. False
13. True
14. True
15. True
16. False
17. False
18. False
19. True
20. True

INTRODUCTION TO DUAL DIAGNOSIS (MENTAL HEALTH/BEHAVIORALDISORDERS IN PERSON WITH MENTAL RETARDATION)

REFERENCES

American Psychiatric Association (1994). *Diagnostic and statistical manual of mental disorders* (4th edition). Washington, DC: Author.

Elliott, F. A. (1984). The episodic dyscontrol syndrome. *Neurologic Clinics, 2,* 113-125.

Gualtieri, C., Quade, D., Hicks, R., Mayo, J., & Schroeder, S. (1984). Tardive dyskinesia and other clinical consequences of neuroleptic treatment in children and adolescents. *American Journal of Psychiatry, 141,* 20-33.

Hardman, J. G., Limbird, L. E., Molinoff, P. B., Ruddon, R. W., & Gilman, A. G. (Eds.) (1996). *Goodman and Gilman's The pharmaceutical basis of therapeutics.* New York: McGraw-Hill.

Lawson, W. B. & Karson, C. N. (1994). Clinical correlates of body weight changes in schizophrenia. *Journal of Neuropsychiatry, 6,* 187-188.

Poindexter, A. R., Berglund, J. A., & Kolstoe, P. D. (1993). Changes in antiepileptic drug prescribing patterns in large institutions: Preliminary results of a five-year experience. *American Journal on Mental Retardation, 98 (suppl.),* 776-780.

Poindexter, A. R. (1994, Nov.). Weight changes associated with neuroleptic withdrawal. *NADD Newsletter,* 7-8.

Schatzberg, A. F. & Cole, J. O. (1991). *Manual of clinical psychopharmacology.* Washington, DC: American Psychiatric Press.

Sovner, R. & Hurley, A. D. (1982). Hydrocephalus and the cocktail party syndrome. *Psychiatric Aspects of Mental Retardation Newsletter, 1,* 13-16.

Sovner, R. & Hurley, A. D. (1983). Preparing for a mental health consultation. *Psychiatric Aspects of Mental Retardation Newsletter, 2,* 37-40.

Sovner, R. & Hurley, A. D. (1986). Four non-specific factors associated with mental retardation which influence the process of making a psychiatric diagnosis. *Psychiatric Aspects of Mental Retardation Reviews, 5,* 45-50.

Volavka, J. (1995). *Neurobiology of violence.* Washington, DC: American Psychiatric Press.

DEPRESSION IN PERSONS WITH MENTAL RETARDATION

Instructions for use of this self-directed instruction program:

- Cover the right-hand side of each page, since this gives the answer to the questions.
- Read each section carefully, and WRITE your answer in the designated place.
- After WRITING your answer, check and see if you are correct.
- Refer to your handout materials as necessary.

DEPRESSION IN PERSONS WITH MENTAL RETARDATION

Depression is a common type of mental illness, affecting an estimated ten million or more people in the United States every year. Up to one in eight individuals may require treatment of depression during their lifetimes. Depression is a (rare or common?) type of mental illness. ____________

common

Several recent large studies suggest that depression is increasing, particularly in people born since World War II. Also, the age of onset seems to be decreasing, with new cases often developing in late teenage and early adult years. The incidence of depression seems to be (increasing or decreasing?), particularly in younger persons and in anyone born since World War II. ____________________

increasing

Women are two to three times more apt to develop depression, across all age groups. Women are (more or less?) apt to have depression than men. _______________

more (This and other trends only occur in western countries, and not in other parts of the world.)

While the cause of depression is unknown, it seems to be the result of interplay between many factors. It tends to run in families, which indicates some genetic influence, especially in severe cases. Depression also seems to be more common in people who are poor, and in unmarried men. There (seems to be or seems not to be?) a genetic component to depression. ___________________

seems to be

Depression often develops after severely stressful life events, so both circumstances and heredity seem to be often be involved at the beginning of an episode of depression. An unmarried man whose mother dies suddenly, and whose sister has a history of depression, may develop depression both because of factors of h_______________ and because of his life circumstances.

heredity (Unmarried men are more apt to develop depression than married me, and loss of a parent is a stressful life event.)

The American Psychiatric Association has developed a list of nine symptoms of major depression, five of which must have been present during the same two-week period and which must represent a change from previous function. According to the APA, ______ of the nine listed symptoms must be present to make a diagnosis of major depressive illness.

Five

To make a diagnosis, symptoms of depression must cause clinically significant distress or impairment of social, occupational, or other areas of functioning. A diagnosis of depression (can or cannot?) be made in a person who seems to function well both at home, at work, and during recreational activities. ___________________

cannot

At least ONE of TWO of the nine symptoms must be present for diagnosis: 1) depressed mood most of the day, most days, either by own report or report of others and/or 2) markedly diminished interest or pleasure in all, or almost all, activities most of the time, by own report or report of others. A sad mood and/or significant loss of interest (is or isn't?) required to make a diagnosis, along with enough other symptoms to make a total of at least five. _________________

is

In children or adolescents, the depressed mood may be irritable. Depressed people with mental retardation may have a sad expression, many complaints of feeling bad, withdraw from others, or may become aggressive. Children who are depressed may appear _______________ rather than sad.

irritable (or aggressive)

All but which one of the following may be symptoms of depression in people with mental retardation?: a) banging their own head; b) happy, satisfied facial expression; c) decreased spells of aggression toward others; d) complaints of headache; or e) refusal to attend recreational activities. ____________

b) (As a depressed person becomes more withdrawn, he/she may become less aggressive due to less contact with others.)

A person who is depressed may have 3) significant weight loss or weight gain, when not intentionally dieting, with a weight change of 5% or more in a month, or significant increase or decrease of appetite nearly every day. A 10-year old child whose weight has remained unchanged for two years (does or doesn't?) have one depression symptom. ________________

does (Children with depression may not actually lose weight, but may instead fail to makeexpected gains associated with gains in height.)

Appetite disturbances in people with mental retardation may be best assessed by monitoring weight changes carefully. Appetite changes in an individual with mental retardation are most easily checked by carefully watching his/her __________________.

weight

Persons with depression may have 4) *insomnia* (too little sleep) or *hypersomnia* (too much sleep) nearly every day. The term "hypersomnia" means (too much or too little?) sleep. _______________

too much

Sleep disturbances in depressed people with mental retardation may present as unruly behavior at bedtime or during the night, and/ or by excessive sleep during scheduled program activities the day after a night of insomnia. Insomnia may be suspected in a person with mental retardation if he/she is (sleepy or very alert?) during activities at the workplace. ____________________

sleepy (Sleepiness during the daytime may also be a symptom of hypersomnia as well as insomnia.)

The relationship of sleep patterns to depression is difficult to evaluate in blind persons, since these individuals may have atypical sleep patterns associated with their blindness. These atypical sleep patterns are usually cyclic in nature, and are the result of trouble adjusting to a "normal" 24-hour light/dark cycle. People who cannot see light (often or seldom?) have atypical sleep patterns. ________________

often

A person who increases body weight from 150 to 160 pounds in one month, and begins to have difficulty awakening in the morning, even when bedtime is 9:00 PM, (meets or does not meet?) criteria for two symptoms of depression. ____________________

meets

A depressed person may have 5) either agitated or slowed physical movements, as compared to their usual physical activity, as observable by others nearly every day. Reports by the person of feelings of restlessness or of being "slowed down" do not meet criteria for these symptoms. Self-reports of psychomotor agitation (do or don't?) meet criteria for depression. ______________

don't

Psychomotor changes such as agitated or slowed physical movements may present as a behavior disorder of recent onset in persons with mental retardation. Increased agitation and episodes of aggress (may be or probably aren't?) psychomotor changes associated with depression in people with mental retardation. ____________

may be

An individual with depression may 6) complain of fatigue or lack of energy, with symptoms occurring nearly every day. A person with depression usually (does or doesn't?) appear to be energetic and enthusiastic about daily activities. ____________

doesn't

Symptoms such as fatigue or lack of energy may show up as a decrease in work productivity in a depressed person with mental retardation. An individual with mental retardation who has a major depression may be expected to (decrease or maintain?) usual production levels in his/her work setting. ____________

decrease (Changes in production back toward usual levels may be a marker of successful treatment or spontaneous remission of depression.)

A person with depression often 7) reports feelings of worthlessness or excessive or inappropriate guilt nearly every day. (Self-reproach or guilt about being sick do not in themselves serve to meet criteria for this symptom.) A depressed person with mental retardation may make statements such as "I'm dumb—stupid—no one likes me." Occasional feeling of worthlessness (meet or do not meet?) criteria for a symptom of major depression. ____________

do not meet

A person with depression may have 8) diminished ability to think or concentrate and/or may have trouble making decisions, nearly every day, as reported by self or others. A person with mental retardation who is depressed may have an IQ decrease as compared to earlier testing, or may have a decrease in attention span. An individual who appears sad and whose measured IQ has gone from 65 to 50 in a year (may be or is not apt to be?) depressed.

____

may be

While almost anyone may have a fear of dying, a person with depression may have 9) recurrent thoughts of death and/or suicide, and may plan or actually attempt suicide. Risk of suicide serves to make depression a potentially life-threatening disorder. A fear of dying probably (is or isn't?) a symptom of depression. ___________

isn't (Almost everyone has some fear of dying.)

A person with mental retardation who has had increased sleeplessness at night, frequent complaints of worthlessness, and has had decreased production in the workshop meets criteria for how many symptoms of the American Psychiatric Association diagnostic system for major depression?_____________

two (Decreased work production may be a result of daytime sleepiness secondary to insomnia, rather than a symptom in itself.)

An individual with depression may characteristically have all but which one of the following symptoms: weight change from 150 to 142 pounds in a 3-week period; trouble making decisions; no particular impairment in functioning areas; frequent appearance of tearfulness despite denying any distress; avoidance of the company of others (behavior change). ___________________

______________________________.

no particular impairment in functioning areas (If no impairment is present, no diagnosis can be made.)

Symptoms of depression may be associated with some medical conditions such as *hypothyroidism* (low thyroid function), as well as some kinds of medications. If a person looks depressed and has a general medical condition at the same time which may be causing the depression, usually the general medical condition is treated first. A person has untreated hypothyroidism and six symptoms of depression. Which condition should probably be treated first? ______________________

hypothyroidism

If depressive symptoms persist after the hypothyroidism is adequately treated, treatment for depression is (probably or probably not?) indicated. ______________________

probably

If medication being used for a general medical condition seems to be causing symptoms of depression, the medication regimen should be modified if possible. Then, if symptoms of depression persist, the depression should be treated. If an individual is receiving medication for a general medical condition that appears to be causing symptoms of depression, (change of medication or treatment of depressive symptoms?) should be attempted first.

________________ ________________.

hange of medication (if at all possible)

Some classes of drugs that commonly cause depression include beta blockers, centrally acting antihypertensives, steroids, and barbiturates. All but which one of the following have been reported to cause symptoms of depression?: Inderal™ (propranolol, a beta blocker); Tegretol™ (carbamazepine, an antiepileptic); Catapres™ (clonidine, a centrally acting antihypertensive); phenobarbital.

____

Tegretol™ (While carbamazepine is an antiepileptic drug as is phenobarbital, it is not a barbiturate.)

Diagnosis of a major depressive episode is not usually made if symptoms begin within two months of the loss of a loved one, unless symptoms are associated with marked functional impairment, morbid preoccupation with worthlessness, suicidal thoughts, psychotic symptoms such as hallucinations, or psychomotor retardation. Severe symptoms of depression with the loss of a loved one (may or probably don't?) indicate a diagnosis of depressive illness. ______________

may

Persons with mental retardation may perceive staff changes as loss of a loved one. If depressive symptoms persist or significantly interfere with function, treatment may be indicated. A man with mental retardation who lives in a group home usually appears happy. After moving to his own apartment he becomes sad and withdrawn, and cries frequently at the place where he works. He (probably or probably doesn't?) perceive(s) his move as a loss of a loved one or loved ones. ______________

probably (since familiar staff are no longer regularly present)

A woman experiences the death of a child and immediately appears depressed and has markedly decreased interest in her usual daily activities. She cries often, and gains ten pounds in the month after her child's death. She complains of trouble sleeping. A diagnosis of major depressive disorder probably (should or should not?) be made five weeks after the child's death. ______________

should not (unless symptoms are extremely severe, such as being associated with hallucinations, or with marked suicidal tendencies)

In recent years biochemical studies in depression suggest that different brain "chemical messengers" (*neurotransmitters)* may be involved in depressive symptoms in different people. Nonetheless, the original drugs used to treat depression, the tricyclic antidepressants, are still drugs of choice for some people with depression. The original drugs used for depression, still in use today, are the ________________.

tricyclic antidepressants

Some of the tricyclic antidepressants in common use are amitryptiline (Elavil™, Endep™), amoxapine (Asendin™), desipramine (Norpramin™), doxepin (Sinequan™), imipramine (Tofranil™), and nortryptiline (Aventyl™, Pamelor™). Some of these drugs cause drowsiness, and all can cause dry mouth, constipation, and/or weight gain. Common side effects of this group of drugs include which one of these symptoms?: drooling, diarrhea, weight gain

____

weight gain (Constipation and dry mouth frequently occur, and some tricyclics cause drowsiness.)

Another tricyclic drug, used primarily for obsessive-compulsive disorder instead of depression, is clomipramine (Anafranil™). Side effects of Anafranil™ might be expected to include all but which one of the following?: dry mouth, diarrhea, weight gain

____

diarrhea

Newer types of antidepressant drugs, which are not tricyclics, act on different chemical systems in the brain, and thus may have different side effects. Fluoxetine (Prozac™) has common side effects which may include dry mouth, drowsiness, dizziness, weight loss, low blood sodium, and low blood sugar. A very small number of individuals taking Prozac™ have been reported to become suicidal, but this is probably very rare. Prozac™ is typically associated with (weight gain or weight loss?) ________________.

weight loss (possibly)

Maprotiline (Ludiomil™) has common side effects of dry mouth, drowsiness, and dizziness. Phenelzine (Nardil™) has side effects which may include blood pressure problems, constipation, dizziness, and weight gain. Sertraline (Zoloft™) has common side effects of nausea, dry mouth, headache, insomnia, and weight loss. Of the drugs Ludiomil™, Nardil™, and Zoloft™, each has (the same or some differences in?) side effects. ______________________

some differences in

The trade ("brand") name for sertraline is ______________.

Zoloft™

Trazadone (Desyrel™) may cause drowsiness or *priapism*. Priapism is prolonged or inappropriate erection of the penis. Since persons with retardation may not be able to verbally report their symptoms, men with mental retardation who are receiving Desyrel™ should be observed for ______________.

priapism (prolonged or inappropriate erection of the penis)

All drugs have side effects, and certainly the possibility of occurrence of side effects should not prevent a trial of antidepressant medication for persons with mental retardation who are depressed, if that treatment has potential for improving the quality of their lives. Often drug treatment programs can be adjusted to minimize side effects if such occur. Is it true that some medications have no side effects? ________

no (Some have less than others.)

An herbal preparation, St. John's Wort (*hypericum perforatum L.)* seems to show some benefit as an antidepressant, particularly for mild to moderagte depression. Side

effects are probably fewer than with conventional antidepressants, but may include sun sensitivity of the skin, upset stomach, dizziness, dry mouth, sedation, restlessness, and constipation. St. John's Wort also may interact with other drugs, causing side effects of the other drugs. True or false?: Because St. John's Wort is a "natural" herbal preparation, it does not have side effects, and can be used safely with other preparations.
____

false

While medication is often necessary to effectively treat depression, many depressed people do not full respond to, or will not cooperate with, drug trials. Nondrug interventions, such as individual and family education, self-help efforts, cognitive ("talk") therapy, family involvement, and behavioral scheduling may, in different combinations, provide either primary or add-on treatment for mild to moderate depression. Are drugs always necessary?
____

no

Behavioral therapy is not necessarily a less-restrictive treatment than drug therapy, particularly if symptoms of depression are severe and very disabling. Often both medication and behavioral treatment are indicated to achieve optimal relief of symptoms. Behavioral treatment (sometimes or always?) should be tried first, before antidepressant medications.
____

sometimes (Present regulations mandate least-restrictive treatment, but do not preclude drug therapy as initial treatment.)

In addition to antidepressant medication and possibly supportive psychotherapy, new treatments based on behavioral learning theory are now being used. Since abnormal behavior, inadequate social skills, and abnormal thought processes are often a part of depressive symptoms, treatment of these areas is logical, particularly in people with mental retardation. Teaching of new ways of acting, interacting, and thinking (may or won't?) help improve symptoms of depression. ____________

may

Using "operant reinforcement" as a basis for treatment of obvious abnormal behavior, behaviors uncharacteristic of depression are reinforced and behaviors characteristic of depression are not reinforced. Reinforcers are, of course, chose from things the person is known to prefer. As an example, positive answers to the question "Are you happy most of the time?" might be reinforced with an edible treat. Reinforcers should be (standardized or individualized?). ________________________

individualized (according to the person's own demonstrated preferences)

Many of the behaviors characteristic of depression in people with mental retardation are associated with poor social skills. Thus depressed persons may rarely if ever interact in a pleasant, positive manner, and therefor rarely get positive responses from others. Treatment might include finding which social activities seem rewarding, and then teaching ways to increase the number of these activities. Folks with MR (can or can't?) learn to be more pleasant. ____________

can

Since thoughts greatly influence everyone's emotions and behaviors, a number of cognitive-behavioral treatments have been developed for depression. In a depressed person with mental retardation, particularly if he/she has some simple academic skills, a self-monitoring and data recording system can be developed in which he/she reinforces himself/herself for positive progress. More positive thinking (can or doesn't?) improve symptoms of depression. ____________

can

Some ways counselors treat a person with mental retardation and depression include providing supportive, positive relationships, giving on-the-spot corrective feedback and praise for positive behaviors, pointing out successes and "happy" things, and gently challenging negative interpretations of life events, as well as showing different ways of looking at these events. Effective counselors often (give praise for or ignore?) positive attitudes and successes. ______________________________

give praise for

Positive reinforcement for positive behaviors and lack of reinforcement for negative behaviors should not be limited to a formal counseling program, but can easily be made a part of all aspects of the everyday life of an individual with mental retardation and depression. Direct support staff (should or shouldn't?) try to reinforce positive thoughts in the individuals they serve. ______________________

should (without in any way attempting to minimize the discomfort of the affected individual, of course)

Any treatment can produce unpleasant side effects, including behavioral treatment. "Bad" behavior may increase because the person cannot tolerate the anxiety associated with treatment. Target symptoms may actually increase, if the individual was getting "secondary gain" (as increased attention) from his/her symptoms. When a man receives reinforcement from the sympathy he gets for his symptoms, he is receiving s_____________ g_____________ from being sick.

secondary gain

A depressed person with mental retardation who has become comfortable with very little socialization may be expected initially (welcome or resent?) social interaction. ________________

resent (perhaps even to the degree of becoming significantly more aggressive)

Cognitive and behavioral therapy should never be viewed as a "less restrictive treatment" which should always be tried prior to the use of antidepressant drugs. Sometimes behavioral therapy is the treatment of choice, sometimes drugs are the most appropriate first intervention. Some people need both forms of treatment. Pharmacologic treatments should (always, never, or sometimes?) be the first line of treatment for depression. ________________

sometimes

Diagnosis of depression is often missed in persons with mental retardation who are quiet, or who become quieter than usual. An individual who is usually active or even hyperactive who becomes quieter and whose "target behaviors" go down is not necessarily better—he/she may be developing depression. Any such changes should be carefully evaluated. An aggressive man with mental retardation whose aggressive episodes decrease (is or may not be?) "improved." ________________

may not be

A woman with mental retardation and depression whose depressive symptoms include increased withdrawal and quietness has a marked increase in numbers of minor aggressive episodes when treated with Zoloft™ for her depression. This finding probably (does or does not?) require a change in her Zoloft dosage, or the addition of some other psychotropic drug. ________________

does not (This probably is not an adverse drug reaction, but is apt to be the result of more interactions with people in her environment.)

Persons who work with individuals with mental retardation on a day-to-day basis are in the best position to suspect early symptoms of depression in those people they serve. Their knowledge of the symptoms of depression is extremely important, since this diagnosis may be difficult to make in this population. Family doctors and even psychiatrists (seldom or often?) have trouble making a diagnosis of depression in people with mental retardation.

often (Information provided by those who work closely with people with mental retardation is extremely important for diagnosis-making.)

Since antidepressant treatment is usually of no particular benefit to anyone who is not depressed, and since antidepressant drug treatment and/or psychological treatments often help people with depression, precision of diagnosis is extremely important. antidepressant drug therapy (may or probably doesn't?) benefit aggressive persons with mental retardation, even if they do not have depression.

probably doesn't

Direct support personnel, teachers, work site personnel, family members, and others with frequent contact with people with mental retardation (often or seldom?) have much to offer in facilitating diagnosis of depression.

often

THE END

DEPRESSION IN PERSONS WITH MENTAL RETARDATION

HANDOUT

MAJOR DEPRESSIVE EPISODE

According to Diagnostic and Statistical Manual of Mental Disorders, 4th Edition (DSM-IV), for a diagnosis of depression to be made, at least five symptoms from a list of nine must have been present during the same two-week period. These symptoms must represent a change from the way the person functioned previously. At least one of the five (or more) symptoms must be depressed mood or loss of interest or pleasure in daily activities. Depressed mood may be determined either by reports from the person himself/herself, or from observations made by others. In children and adolescents, and persons with mental retardation, the mood may be irritable rather than obviously depressed. Depressed mood in a person with mental retardation may show up as a sad facial expression, withdrawal, vague physical complaints, onset of aggressive symptoms, and/or regression in behavior.

Other possible symptoms of depression include significant weight loss or weight gain, when not dieting, of five percent or more of body weight in a one-month period, or decrease or increase of appetite almost every day. Children who are depressed may not lose weight, but may fail to make expected weight gains for their gains in height. People with depression often have sleep disorders—either insomnia (not enough sleep) or hypersomnia (too much sleep) nearly every day. Sleep disturbances in people with mental retardation who depressed may show up as disruptive behavior at bedtime or during the night.

People with depression may be noted to have either increased body movement activity (psychomotor agitation) or decreased body movement activity (psychomotor retardation) nearly every day, as observed by others. Psychomotor agitation in a person with mental retardation may present as a behavior problem of recent onset. Psychomotor retardation may show up as a change in productivity/performance at their day program or vocational site. People with depression often complain of being tired a lot or having a loss of energy.

People with depression often complain of feelings of worthlessness or excessive, inappropriate guilt. This guilt may be as extreme as being delusional, and does not involve merely self-reproach about being sick. Persons with mental retardation who are depressed may express these feelings in statements such as "I'm dumb—stupid—no one likes me—"

Persons with depression also may have decreased ability to think or concentrate, and may appear indecisive. (These symptoms may be reported by the individual or by others.) In people with mental retardation, cognitive (thought) disturbances associated with depression may show up as a decrease in IQ or functional ability when re-tested, or by change in attention span while performing their usual activities. People with depression often have recurrent thoughts of death or dying, and may either think a lot about suicide, plan suicide, or make suicide attempts. People with mental retardation also may have these thoughts/plans/attempts.

To make a diagnosis of depression, the symptoms must cause the person clinically significant distress, and/or must impair social, occupational, or other important areas of functioning. Symptoms due to direct effects of a substance, such as medications or drugs of abuse, or general medical conditions, should not be counted in making a diagnosis of major depression. A diagnosis of depression is generally not made if symptoms occur within two months of the loss of a loved one, unless symptoms are associated with marked functional impairment, morbid preoccupation with worthlessness, suicidal thoughts, symptoms of psychosis, or marked psychomotor retardation.

References:

American Psychiatric Association. (1994). Diagnostic and statistical manual of mental disorders (4th ed.). Washington, DC: Author.

Hurley, A. D. (1998). Two cases of suicide attempt by patients with Down's syndrome. Psychiatric Services, 49, 1618-1619.

DEPRESSION IN PERSONS WITH MENTAL RETARDATION

REFERENCES

Agency for Health Care Policy and Research. (1993). *Depression in primary care: Volume 1. Detection and diagnosis* (AHCPR Publication #93-0550). Washington, DC: U.S. Govt. Printing Office.

American Psychiatric Association (1994). *Diagnostic and statistical manual of mental disorders* (4th ed.). Washington, DC: Author.

Berenbaum, I. L. (1985, Jan. 30). Unmasking clinical depression: When to refer. *Hospital Practice.*

Calvocoressi, L., Libman, D., Vegso, S. J., McDougle, C. J., & Price, L.H. (1998). Global functioning of inpatients with obsessive-compulsive disorder, schizophrenia, and major depression. *Psychiatric Services, 49,* 379-381.

Charlot, L. R. (1997). Irritability, aggression, and depression in adults with mental retardation: A developmental perspective. *Psychiatric Annals, 27,* 190-197.

Council on Scientific Affairs, American Medical Association (1993). The etiologic features of depression in adults. *Archives of Family Medicine, 2,* 76-83.

El-Mallakh, R. S., Wright, J. C., Breen, K. J., & Lippmann, S. B. (1996). Clues to depression in primary care practice. *Postgraduate Medicine, 100,* 85-96.

Hurley, A. D. (1998). Two cases of suicide attempt by patients with Down's syndrome. *Psychiatric Services, 49,* 1618-1619.

Hurley, A. D. & Sovner, R. (1991). Cognitive behavioral therapy for depression in individuals with developmental disabilities. *Habilitative Mental Healthcare Newsletter, 10,* 41-47.

Jefferson, J. W. (1992). Antidepressant side effects and their treatment. *Cliniguide to Depression in Primary Care, 1,* issue 2.

Klerman, G. L. & Weissman, M. M. (1989). Increasing rates of depression. *Journal of the American Medical Association, 261,* 2229-2235.

Lebowitz, B. D., Pearson, J. L., Schneider, L. S., Reynolds, C. F., Alexopoulos, G. S., Bruce, M. L., Conwell, Y., Katz, I. R., Meyers, B. S., Morrison, M. F., Mossey, J., Niederehe, G., & Parmelee, P. (1997). Diagnosis and treatment of depression in late life: Consensus statement update. *Journal of the American Medical Association, 278,* 1186-1190.
Marston, G. M., Perry, D. W., & Roy, A. (1997). Manifestations of de-

pression in people with intellectual disability. *Journal of Intellectual Disability Research, 41,* 476-480.

Matson, J. I. (1983). Depression in the mentally retarded: Toward a conceptual analysis of diagnosis. *Progress in Behavior Modification, 15,* 57-79.

NIH Consensus Development Panel on Depression in Late Life (1992). Diagnosis and treatment of depression in late life. *Journal of the American Medical Association, 268,* 1018-1024.

Pary, R. J. (1997). What is the short-term effect of depression on adaptive behavior?. *habilitative Mental Healthcare Newsletter, 16,* 48-49.

Rush, A. J. (1993). Depression in primary care: Detection, diagnosis, and treatment. *American Family Physician, 47,* 1776-1788.

Potter, W. Z., Rudorfer, M. V., & Manji, H. (1991). The pharmacologic treatment of depression. *New England Journal of Medicine, 325,* 633-642.

Pyne, J. M., Patterson, T. L., Kaplan, R. M., Gillin, J. C., Koch, W. L.,& Grant, I. (1997). Assessment of the quality of life of patients with major depression. *Psychiatric Services, 48,* 224-230.

Rowe, M.G., Fleming, M. F., Barry, K. L., Manwell, L. B., & Kropp, S. (1995). Correlates of depression in primary care. *Journal of Family Practice, 41,* 551-558.

Settle, E. C. (1993, July). Managing antidepressant side effects. *Drug Therapy.*

Settle, E. C. (1993, Sept.). Side effects of antidepressant medications. *Pharmacy and Therapeutics.*

Shearer, S. I. & Adams, G. K. (1993). Nonpharmacologic aids in the treatment of depression. *American Family Physician, 47,* 435-441.

Simpson, S. G. & DePaulo, J. R. (1993). Are you recognizing depression in your patients?. *Postgraduate Medicine, 94,* 85-93.

Sovner, R., Hurley, A. D., & LaBrie, R. A. (1982). Diagnosing depression in the mentally retarded. *Psychiatric Aspects of Mental Retardation Newsletter, 1,* 1-4.

Wong, A. H. C., Smith, M., & Boon, H. (1998). Herbal remedies in psychiatric practice. *Archives of General Psychiatry, 55,* 1033-1044.

Zal, H. M. (1994, March). Depression in the elderly: Differing presentations, wide choice of therapies. *Consultant.*

DEPRESSION IN PERSONS WITH MENTAL RETARDATION

Educational Objectives

Participants will be able to answer the following questions:

1. What diagnostic criteria are necessary to make a diagnosis of depression?
2. How are symptoms of depression made manifest in persons with mental retardation?
3. What types of treatment are usually effective for persons with depression?
4. What are common side effects for medications commonly prescribed for depression?
5. How can members of interdisciplinary teams serving people with mental retardation facilitate diagnosis and treatment of depression in this population?

DEPRESSION IN PERSONS WITH MENTAL RETARDATION

Pretest/Posttest

T F 1. Recent studies show that depression is becoming more common in persons born before 1940.

T F 2. Unmarried men are more apt to have depression than married men.

T F 3. In general, depression does not cause much functional impairment.

T F 4. Most people with major depression are correctly recognized by primary health care providers.

T F 5. Depression is seen in about 10% of nursing home residents.

T F 6. Either a depressed mood or significant loss of interest in usual activities is required to make a diagnosis of depression.

T F 7. Being sad means that one has depression.

T F 8. Children who are depressed may appear irritable rather than sad.

T F 9. Weight gain may be a symptom of depression.

T F 10. A person with mental retardation and depression may have a decreased incidence of aggression toward others.

T F 11. People with depression may sleep too much or sleep too little.

T F 12. Depression may be readily diagnosed in blind persons by analyzing sleep patterns.

T F 13. Occasional feelings of worthlessness are not particularly significant in diagnosing depression.

T F 14. Persons with mental retardation and depression often have a measured increase in IQ.

T F 15. Low thyroid function is often associated with symptoms of depression.

T F 16. Propranolol (Inderal™) has been associated with symptoms of depression.

T F 17. Tricyclic antidepressant drugs often make people drool.

T F 18. Priapism means prolonged ringing of the ears.

T F 19. Behavioral therapy is a less-restrictive treatment than medication and should always be tried first.

T F 20. When people with mental retardation and depression are treated, their counted target behaviors may increase.

T F 21. Input from direct care staff and others who know people with mental retardation well is very important in making a diagnosis of depression.

Name: ________________________ Position: ____________________

Date: ___________________

DEPRESSION IN PERSONS WITH MENTAL RETARDATION

Pretest/Posttest Answers

1. false
2. true
3. false
4. false
5. false
6. true
7. false
8. true
9. true
10. true
11. true
12. false
13. true
14. false
15. true
16. true
17. false
18. false
19. false
20. true
21. true

ANXIETY DISORDERS AND RELATED CONDITIONS

Instructions for use of this self-directed instruction program:

- Cover the right-hand side of each page, since this gives the answer to the questions.
- Read each section carefully, and WRITE your answer in the designated place.
- After WRITING your answer, check and see if you are correct.
- Refer to your handout materials as necessary.

ANXIETY DISORDERS AND RELATED CONDITIONS

Anxiety disorders are the most common mental health disorders seen by primary care physicians. The typical primary care doctor sees at least one person with an anxiety disorder in his/her office every day. The characteristic features of this group of disorders include symptoms of *anxiety* and *avoidance* behavior. True or false?: Physicians rarely see patients with anxiety disorder(s).

____

false

While depression and anxiety disorders have some symptoms in common, and certainly may occur in the same person, the features more characteristic of anxiety include:

- Trouble falling asleep
- Avoidance behavior based on fear
- Rapid pulse
- Breathing difficulties
- Apprehension (fearfulness)
- Tremors
- Heart palpitations
- Sweating
- Hot or cold spells
- Dizziness

Another symptom often associated with anxiety disorders is the feeling of detachment from all or parts of one's body (depersonalization). Sometimes people who have anxiety disorders also have the sensation that the immediate environment is strange, unreal, or unfamiliar (derealization). Some medications, such as asthma medications, can cause symptoms similar to anxiety disorders, and some general medical conditions such as over-active thyroid gland can also do so. True or false?: It is possible to have an over-active thyroid gland and present with symptoms which resemble an anxiety disorder. __________

True

A *panic attack* can occur in a variety of anxiety disorders. This is not a diagnosis, but is a group of symptoms occurring during a discrete period of intense fear or discomfort. The *Diagnostic and Statistical Manual of Mental Disorders, Fourth Edition* (DSM-IV) lists 13 of these symptoms, four of which must be present, develop abruptly, and reach a peak within ten minutes:

1. Palpitations
2. Sweating
3. Trembling or shaking
4. Shortness of breath or sensation of smothering
5. Feeling of choking
6. Chest pain or discomfort
7. Nausea or abdominal distress
8. Feeling dizzy or faint
9. *Derealization* (feelings of unreality) and/or *depersonalization* (feeling detached from oneself)
10. Fear of losing control or going crazy
11. Fear of dying
12. Paresthesias (numbness or tingling sensations)
13. Chills or hot flashes.

True or false?: Panic attacks may be associated with physical discomfort. __________

True

Which of the following is **not** a part of the criteria for panic attack?: __________

a) trembling
b) chest pain
c) headache
d) fear

c) headache

Agoraphobia means anxiety about being in places or situations from which escape might be difficult or embarrassing, or in which help might not be available if an unexpected panic attack occurs. People who have agoraphobia may refuse to leave their home because of fear of a panic attack. To make a diagnosis of panic disorder without agoraphobia, the person must have recurrent, unexpected panic attacks. At least one attack should be followed by a month or more of persistent concern about having more attacks, worry about implications of the attack or its consequences, and/or a significant behavior change related to the attacks. Some prescribed drugs, drugs of abuse, or hyperthyroidism (excessive thyroid function) may present with symptoms similar to symptoms of a panic attack. True or false?: One sign of agoraphobia is the affected person's worry about having more panic attacks.

True

A specific *phobia* is defined as a marked and persistent fear of a specific object or situation. Examples are fear of flying, heights, animals, receiving an injection ("shot"), and seeing blood. Exposure to the specific object or situation usually provokes an immediate anxiety response, which often takes the form of a panic attack. In children, panic associated with a phobia may be expressed by crying, tantrums, freezing, or clinging. Persons with mental retardation may react in similar fashion, or may become aggressive to get away from the feared situation. Adults with phobias typically recognize that the fear is excessive or unreasonable, but people who have MR and children may not recognize that the fear is irrational or excessive. In a true phobia, the avoidance, anxious anticipation, or distress in the feared situations interferes significantly with normal routine, functioning, social activities, or relationships with others, or there is marked distress about having the phobia. Trivial fears, such as fear about flying which only involves the tight gripping of the armrests on takeoff and landing do not meet criteria for a phobic disorder. Which of the following answers is true for this question: While on vacation to the Grand Canyon, a person avoids walking too close to the edge of cliffs. Based on this fact alone, he/she has ________

a) a phobia of heights
b) no diagnosable problem
c) agoraphobia
d) problems with social functioning

b) no diagnosable problem

True or false?: The impact of a specific phobia on the affected person's overall life helps determine whether he/she may receive this diagnosis. ____________

True

Many people with anxiety have *generalized anxiety disorder,* in which they have excessive anxiety and worry about a number of events or activities. For this be diagnosable, they must have symptoms more days than not, for at least six months. The individual with generalized anxiety disorder finds it very hard to control his/her worry. Symptoms that may be associated with generalized anxiety disorder include:

- restlessness
- easy fatigability
- trouble concentrating
- irritability
- muscle tension
- sleep disturbance (trouble falling or staying asleep or restless, unsatisfying sleep)

The anxiety, worry, and/or physical symptoms of generalized anxiety disorder cause clinically significant distress or impairment in social, occupational, or other important areas of functioning. True or false?: It is easy to control the symptoms of generalized anxiety disorder. __________

false

True or false?: If a person worries a lot and seems "stressed," but only about his/her job and nothing else, he/she may meet the criteria for generalized anxiety disorder. __________

false

Obsessive-compulsive disorder (OCD) is an anxiety disorder in which either obsessions or compulsions must be present. *Obsessions* are defined as recurrent and persistent thoughts, impulses, or images that are experienced, at some time during the disturbance, as intrusive and inappropriate, and cause marked anxiety or distress. Thoughts, impulses, or images associated with obsessions re not simply excessive worries about real-life problems. The affected person tries to ignore or suppress these thoughts or images, or tries to neutralize them with some other thought or action. As an example, a person who is a "worrier" and who continually talks about problems they have with their children probably does not meet the criteria for OCD. A person with OCD recognizes that the obsessive thoughts, impulses, or images are a product of his/her own mind, and are not the result of someone or something else causing them. Children and people who have mental retardation may not understand this. As an example, an individual who has mental retardation that feels that he must wash his hands until they bleed because he feels he is unclean would probably meet the criteria for

OCD. *Compulsions* are defined as repetitive behaviors (such as hand washing, ordering, checking) or mental acts (meditation, counting) that the person feels driven to perform in response to an obsession. These typically "need" to be done according to strict rules that the person has established, consciously or unconsciously, for himself/herself. All of these rules or behaviors are aimed at preventing or reducing distress or preventing some dreaded event—and controlling the obsessions. True or false?: Obsessions are recurrent, persistent thoughts that cause stress or anxiety. ____________

True

True or false?: If a man washes his hands until they bleed because he insists that the devil is telling him that he is poisoning the CIA, the man probably has obsessive-compulsive disorder. __________

false

Which one of the following answers is correct to complete this statement?: Compulsions are ________________ acts performed by a person in order to manage an obsessive thought.

a) constant
b) rare
c) repetitive
d) random

c) repetitive

There are types of compulsions called *completeness/ incompleteness* compulsions. These include a wide variety of things which "finish" or complete a task—even if the affected person has to "re-do" the task just to finish it. Examples for people with mental retardation include:

- insisting on closing open doors
- taking all items out of a storage area
- removing items and then returning them, over and over
- trying to empty all toiletry bottles in bathroom
- putting on and taking off clothing over and over
- insisting on doing a certain chore (not letting anyone else do it)

These kinds of behavior in a person with intellectual disability would probably assist in making a diagnosis of OCD. True or false?: Completeness/incompleteness compulsions involve finishing tasks, even when re-doing the task is unnecessary. ___________

True

Cleaning/tidiness compulsions may include:

- insisting on doing hygiene steps in a fixed sequence
- cleaning body parts excessively
- insisting on picking up scraps of paper off the ground
- picking at loose threads continuously
- ripping clothes if not prevented
- insisting that a certain activity be done
- hiding or hoarding particular objects

Which one of the following answers is true for this question?: Cleaning/tidiness compulsions are exhibited by all of the following except: ___________________

a) cleaning excessively
b) insisting on closing doors
c) picking at loose threads continuously
d) hiding or hoarding particular objects

b) insisting on closing doors

Checking / touching compulsions include:

- opening and cupboard door and then closing it, over and over
- touching or tapping an item repeatedly
- going through a touching or stepping patter
- unusual sniffing

(Some people with autism appear to go through some of these same rituals.)

Deviant grooming compulsions include:

- picking at hands/face/legs, etc. to the point of gouging skin
- checking self in a mirror excessively
- inappropriate hair cutting
- pulling out hair while sitting calmly

(When working with people with mental retardation, it is important to determine the number and types of compulsions and categories in which symptoms are present.) Which one of the following answers completes this question?: Tapping an item repeatedly is indicative of ________________ compulsions.

a) deviant grooming
b) completeness/incompleteness
c) checking/touching
d) cleaning/tidiness

c) checking/touching

Counting symptoms is often performed using one of several existing checklists, such as the "Compulsive Behavior Checklist." Then, based on data, an assessment of the amount of interference with daily should be made. One determination is to note if the compulsions take more than one hour/day if not prevented, and if they significantly interfere with the person's "normal" routine. Another important part of the Compulsive Behavior Checklist involves a measurement of the response by the involved person when the compulsions are interrupted. Examples of these responses may include:

- stopping momentarily, then resuming activity
- waiting until the observer is gone, then resuming
- becoming angry and aggressive toward the person who intervenes
- biting or hitting self
- head-banging

True or false?: It is unimportant to know what a person does after his/her compulsive behavior is interrupted by someone else. ____________

false

Post-traumatic stress disorder (PTSD) is an anxiety disorder in which the involved person has been exposed to a traumatic event in which the following were present:

- experiencing, witnessing, or being confronted with a situation that involved actual or threatened death or serious injury to self or others
- the individual's response must have involved intense fear, helplessness, or horror

Examples might include a person who comes close to death by fire or someone who has been sexually abused—either of these may develop PTSD. Also, in post-traumatic stress disorder the traumatic event is persistently re-experienced. This can happen in a variety of ways, including:

- recurrent and intrusive recollections of the event ("flashbacks")
- recurrent, distressing dreams of the event
- acting or feeling as if the event were re-

curring
- intense psychological distress to cues symbolizing the event (such as odors associated with the event)
- physical symptoms on exposure to cues of the event

People who have PTSD have persistent avoidance of stimuli associated with the trauma, and have numbing of general responsiveness. These symptoms may present as efforts to avoid thoughts, feelings, or conversations associated with the trauma, efforts to avoid situations or people that cause memories of the trauma, and/or inability to recall facts about the trauma. Other manifestations of PTSD may include:

- decreased interest or participation in significant activities
- feelings of detachment or estrangement from others
- inability to have loving feelings
- a sense of a foreshortened future—not expecting to have a normal life span

Individuals with PTSD also have persistent symptoms of increased arousal such as:

- trouble falling or staying asleep
- irritability or outbursts of anger
- difficulty concentrating
- hypervigilance
- exaggerated startle reflex

An example might be a person who has mental retardation who always keeps his back to the wall when he is in a room with others, and watches everyone around him very closely. He may be demonstrating hypervigilance. To make a diagnosis of post-traumatic stress disorder, the duration of the disturbance must be more than one month and persist for six or more months after the traumatic event occurred. The disturbance must also clause clinically significant distress or impairment in important areas of functioning. True or false?: A person can have post-traumatic stress disorder without ever having been exposed to a traumatic event. __________

false

Which of the following answers is true for this question?: An individual was once the victim of a violent attack in a secluded parking lot at sunset. Based on this, this person may later start to avoid: __________________

a) parking lots
b) being in secluded areas
c) being out at sunset
d) any of the above

d) any of the above

Most types of anxiety disorders are long-term problems. The goal of any kind of treatment is to decrease symptoms to a manageable level. Total elimination of symptoms may not be possible. When people have relatively mild symptoms, usually related to stress, non-drug treatments often are satisfactory, and should be tried first. If symptoms of anxiety disorders are especially severe or persistent, some combination of drugs and non-drug treatments may be required. (Medication treatment of anxiety disorders is covered more fully later in this course.) True or false?: The goal of treatment of psychiatric disorders is to make the person with the diagnosis completely normal. __________

false

The first step in management of anxiety symptoms is evaluation of possible causes. Physical causes of anxiety symptoms should be ruled out first. After physical causes, such as the effects of medication and thyroid disorder, are ruled out, then any connections with daily activities and life circumstances should be carefully explored. True or false?: As is the case with all psychiatric disorders, physical causes of anxiety disorders should be ruled out prior to beginning treatment. ________

True

Life circumstances and daily activities that seem to be contributing to symptoms of anxiety should be corrected or modified if this is possible. After medical causes have been ruled out or corrected and possible corrections of life circumstances are made, treatments such as learning relaxation techniques or biofeedback may be started. Exercise may be helpful for many people with generalized anxiety disorder, and often this is included in an overall treatment plan. Which of the following answers is true for this question?: Which of the following forms of treatment is not used for anxiety disorders?: ________________

a) modification of the person's environment
b) relaxation techniques
c) surgery
d) exercise

c) surgery

Systematic desensitization is usually felt to be the most effective form of treatment for almost everyone with significant simple phobias. Systematic desensitization is a gradually increasing exposure to the feared situation. As the person is gradually exposed to the situation that has caused the phobic reaction, they are also learning, with the help of others, how to manage their emotions and behavior. Eventually, when the person is exposed to the situation which has caused anxiety in the past, they do not respond with anxiety, because they either no longer fear the situation or they have learned to manage the situation to prevent problems. True or false?:

Systematic desensitization is considered the most effective form of treatment for most people with simple phobias. __________ | True

Benzodiazepine drugs such as Librium™, Valium™, Tranxene™, Ativan™, and Xanax™ (all trade names) are the most common drugs prescribed for the treatment of anxiety disorders. The most common side effect for this group of drugs is drowsiness, but some people develop a disinhibiting reaction, which means that the drug makes it more difficult for the person to control his/her own behavior. This type of reaction probably is more common in people with mental retardation than in others. True or false?: The most common side effect of benzodiazepine drugs such as Valium™ and Ativan™ is over-excitement. ____________ | false

Some physical dependence usually develops if people take benzodiazepine drugs for a prolonged period of time. The incidence of dependence and sedation varies from medication to medication. Xanax™, which is among the least sedating of any of these drugs, is said to have the most potential for development of physical dependence. True or false?: Physical dependence is associated with prolonged benzodiazepine treatment. _________ | True

BuSpar™ (buspirone) is a nonsedating antianxiety drug that is not a benzodiazepine. Side effects are rare, but may include headache, nausea, dizziness, and/or tension. Therapeutic effects of BuSpar™ take several weeks to develop, while the therapeutic effects of the benzodiazepine drugs are immediate. Several antidepressant drugs, not usually used for most other anxiety disorders, seem to be particularly effective for OCD. These drugs seem to increase levels of one of the brain chemical messengers, serotonin. Which one of the following answers is true for this question?: Which of the following groups of drugs provides the fastest therapeutic effect?:

____

a) SSRI antidepressants
b) benzodiazepines
c) tricyclic antidepressants
d) all of these are similarly fast-acting

b) benzodiazepines

Of the antidepressant drugs used for OCD, Anafranil™ (clomipramine) is a tricyclic drug whose side effects include dry mouth, weight gain, and constipation. Another type antidepressant drug commonly used for OCD is Prozac™ (fluoxetine). Its common side effects include dry mouth, dizziness, weight loss, low blood sodium, and low blood sugar. True or false?: The trade name for fluoxetine is Prozac™. __________

True

To conclude, people who have mental retardation may have problems with symptoms of anxiety just as do others who do not have obvious disabilities. Due to life experiences, a higher incidence of sexual abuse, and more frequent experience of failure, people who have mental retardation may even be more likely to demonstrate symptoms of anxiety than people in the general population. Direct support staff and others who are knowledgeable about the signs and symptoms of anxiety disorders are of vital importance in making the correct diagnosis, so that appropriate treatment programs can be developed and implemented. True or false?: Direct support staff bear much of the obligation to ensure that people with mental retardation and coexisting anxiety disorders get the treatment they need. __________

True

The End

ANXIETY DISORDERS AND RELATED CONDITIONS

Educational Objectives

Participants in this self-directed instructional program will be able to answer the following questions:

1. What are the most common types of anxiety disorders found both in the general population and in persons with mental retardation?
2. What diagnostic criteria are needed to make a diagnosis of an anxiety disorder?
3. What types of treatment are usually effective for persons with an anxiety disorder?
4. What are common side effects for medications often prescribed for anxiety disorders?
5. How can direct support staff and other members of interdisciplinary teams serving persons with mental retardation facilitate diagnosis and treatment of anxiety disorders in this population?

ANXIETY DISORDERS AND RELATED CONDITIONS

Pretest/Posttest

T F 1. Anxiety disorders are uncommon in the general population, and are not seen often by non-psychiatrist physicians.

T F 2. The term "derealization" defines a sensation that the immediate environment is strange, unreal, or unfamiliar.

T F 3. Symptoms of a panic attack may be mistaken for a heart attach or other serious health problem.

T F 4. Agoraphobia is a technical term which means anxiety about being in places or situations from which escape may be difficult or embarrasing.

T F 5. Symptoms of hyperthyroidism (overactive thyroid gland) may be very similar to those of panic disorder.

T F 6. Trivial fears about flying, involving only tightly gripping armrests on takeoff and landing, meet criteria for a phobic disorder.

T F 7. Individuals with generalized anxiety disorder seldom have trouble concentrating.

T F 8. Some kinds of asthma medicine cause symptoms similar to those of generalized anxiety disorder.

T F 9. Obsessive compulsive disorder (OCD) is an xnxiety disorder in which both obsessions and compulsions must be present.

T F 10. A compulsion is a repetitive behavior or mental act that the person feels driven to perform in rewponse to an obsession or according to rigid rules.

T F 11. A person who is a "worrier" who continually talks about problems they have with their children does not meet criteria for obsessive compulsive disorder.

T F 12. To technically be considered time-consuming, obsessions/ compulsions must take at least one hour per day.

T F 13. Post-traumatic stress disorde is an anxiety disorder in which the involved person has been exposed to a severely traumatic event in which his/her response has involved intense fear, helplessness, or horror.

T F 14. When compulsive activity is interrupted in a person with mental retardation, he/she seldom becomes aggressive.

T F 15. Frightening, intrusive thoughts about an experienced auto wreck may represent post-traumatic stress disorder.

T F 16. An individual with mental retardation who always keeps his back to the wall when he is in a room with others is said to be showing "hypervigilance," which may be a symptom of post-traumatic stress disorder.

T F 17. A diagnosis of post-traumatic stress disorder may be made after one week's worth of symptoms.

T F 18. Goal of treatment of anxiety disorders is to reduce any symp toms to a manageable level.

T F 19. The commonest side effect of benzodiazepine drugs such as Valium™, Ativan™, and Xanax™, is over-excitement.

T F 13. Everyone with a diagnosis of anxiety disorder really needs drug treatment.

Name: ______________________________

Position: ____________________________

Date: _____________________

Answers to Pretest/Posttest on Anxiety Disorders:

1. False
2. True
3. True
4. True
5. True
6. False
7. False
8. True
9. False
10. True
11. True
12. True
13. True
14. False
15. True
16. True
17. False
18. True
19. False
20. False

GENERAL PRINCIPLES OF PSYCHOTIC DISORDERS IN PERSONS WITH MENTAL RETARDATION

Instructions for use of this self-directed instruction program:

- Cover the right-hand side of each page, since this gives the answers to the questions.
- Read each section carefully, and WRITE your answer in the designated place.
- After WRITING your answer, check and see if you are correct.
- Refer to your handout materials as necessary.

GENERAL PRINCIPLES OF PSYCHOTIC DISORDERS IN PERSONS WITH MENTAL RETARDATION

The term *psychosis* has been defined a number of different ways, but very strictly includes only conditions which include *delusions* and/or prominent *hallucinations*. Delusions are incorrect beliefs that usually involve a misinterpretation of perceptions or experiences. If an individual firmly believes that his/her thoughts are controlled by a special radio in his/her head, that person is said to have a d__________________.

delusion

Hallucinations are experienced as hearing, seeing, smelling, tasting, or touching something which is not there. Auditory (hearing) hallucinations are by far the most common type, and are characteristic of *schizophrenia*. When someone hears voices that are not there, he/she is experiencing an auditory h__________________.

hallucination

To be considered a symptom of psychosis, hallucinations must occur in the context of a clear sensorium—the affected individual cannot be just falling asleep or just waking up, for example. True or false?: A person must be "wide awake" when an hallucinations such as hearing voices occurs before an abnormal symptom is diagnosed. ______________

True

People with psychosis usually have very disorganized thinking. Since almost the only way to know what a person is thinking is through what that person says about those thoughts, *disorganization of speech* should be carefully evaluated. Since mildly disorganized speech is common, to be counted as a symptom the disorganization must be obviously severe, and interfere with normal communication. Organization of thought is usually assessed through s________________.

speech

Disorganized behavior associated with psychosis may show itself in a variety of ways, ranging from child-like silliness to unpredictable agitation. Problems may be noted in any form of goal-directed behavior, leading to trouble in performing activities of daily living, such as organizing meals or maintaining personal cleanliness. A person with disorganized behavior due to a psychosis (may not be able to or usually is quite competent to?) organize his/her own daily activities. ________________________________

may not be able to

Grossly disordered behavior must be distinguished from behavior that is just aimless or generally without purpose, and from organized behavior motivated by delusional beliefs. Also, occasional episodes of restless, angry, or agitated behavior shouldn't be considered as evidence of psychosis, especially if the motivation is understandable. A person whose behavior is aimless and drifting (should be or shouldn't be?) considered as having a symptom of psychosis. ____________________

shouldn't be

Catatonic motor behaviors include a marked decrease in reaction to the environment, sometimes reaching an extreme degree of complete unawareness (*catatonic stupor*), maintaining a rigid posture and resisting efforts to be moved (*catatonic rigidity*), or assuming bizarre postures (*catatonic posturing*). A person with psychosis who develops marked decrease in reactivity to his/her environment may be said to be c__________________.

catatonic

Catatonic symptoms are nonspecific and may occur in other mental disorders, such as mood disorders. True or false?: Catatonic stupor is only seen in schizophrenia and other psychotic disorders. ______________

false

While hallucinations and/or delusions may be dramatic, negative symptoms of schizophrenia such as *affective flattening*, *alogia* (inability to speak), and *avolition* (inability to make a decision) may be very disabling. Affective flattening is common, and is characterized by the person's face looking immobile and unresponsive, with poor eye contact and reduced body language. A person who looks blank and unresponsive may be said to have a____________ f____________.

affective flattening

Negative symptoms are hard to evaluate because they are nonspecific (just more severe than normal behaviors), and may be due to a variety of things other than psychosis. Medication side effects, for instance, may look like negative symptoms of psychosis. True or false?: Some medications have side effects similar to symptoms of schizophrenia. ______________

True (Medications such as neuroleptics, which are commonly used to treat psychosis, may have just such effects.)

The distinction between true negative symptoms and medication side effects depends on *clinical judgement*—assessment of the severity of negative symptoms, the nature and type of medication, the effects of dosage adjustment, and the effect(s) of other medications. To tell the difference between drug effects and negative symptoms of psychosis requires c___________ judgement.

clinical

Negative symptoms of schizophrenia may look a lot like symptoms of depression, except people with depression are sad and uncomfortable, while people with psychosis appear more "empty" of feelings. Also, people may learn to be withdrawn and "blank" if they live in a very unstimulating environment. True or false?: People with negative symptoms of schizophrenia look sad and uncomfortable. _______________

false (They usually appear empty of feelings.)

For a diagnosis of schizophrenia to be made, several symptoms must be present together for at least a month, and some signs of disturbance must persist continuously for at least six months. Often less severe symptoms are present before the active phase of the condition (*prodromal symptoms*), and some symptoms may persist after the active phase (*residual symptoms)*. Less severe symptoms present before the active phase begins are called p_________________ symptoms.

prodromal

Diagnosis of psychosis in persons with mental retardation is difficult (but not impossible), since the presence of hallucinations and/or delusions usually is determined by self-report, and many people with mental retardation have problems with communication. True or false?: A diagnosis of psychosis can be made in persons with mental retardation. _______________

True

Also, behaviors often seen in people with moderate or more severe mental retardation may be easily confused with behavioral deficits associated with schizophrenia. Examples include stereotypic behaviors, self-stimulatory behavior, and lack of appropriate social interaction. Persons with mental retardation who have hallucinations may have problems reporting these symptoms because of problems with c________________.

communication

Telling the difference between hallucinations and delusions and other, less serious, symptoms if very important in establishing a correct treatment program for people with mental retardation. A person with mental retardation with hallucinations is more apt to have depression or a significant life stressor than schizophrenia. True or false?: A person with mental retardation may have hallucinations in response to a severe stressful situation. ____________

True

Although a mental health interview may seem rather simple, the ability to be specific, report feelings and abstractions, time frame of symptoms, and history is severely limited in persons with mental retardation. Often, due to *diagnostic overshadowing* (attributing every abnormal behavior to the mental retardation), mental health problems may actually be ignored. Noticing only the mental retardation and not the psychiatric disorder is called d____________ o____________________.

diagnostic overshadowing

Sometimes, instead of missing a psychiatric diagnosis, when people with mental retardation are referred because of behavior problems, a psychiatrist may see the behavior problem as a psychotic disorder, and prescribe antipsychotic drugs , a form of *diagnostic distortion.* In this case depression, anxiety disorders, etc., may be missed, and treatment prescribed for the wrong disorder. True or false?: A person with mental retardation may be over-diagnosed but not under-diagnosed. ________

false (He/she may be either over- or under-diagnosed, due to diagnostic overshadowing or diagnostic distortion.)

During the course of normal development, young children often talk to themselves, engage in solitary fantasy play, and/or invent imaginary friends. These behaviors are also typical of many people with mental retardation who do not have mental illness. A 40-year old man with moderate mental retardation who talks to himself (may very well or probably doesn't?) have a psychosis. ________________

probably doesn't

Persons with mental retardation often have many sorrows and disappointments during their lives. Repeated failures and rejections may often lead to the development of self-gratifying *fantasies*, which may resemble delusions. Any delusions in persons with mental retardation should first be considered as possible fantasy, made worse by unmet need and stress. Self-gratifying fantasies in people with mental retardation often resemble the more serious d__________.

delusions

Sometimes hallucinations and delusions appear in persons in the normal population who aren't psychotic, and certainly this may also happen in people with mental retardation. True or false?: The presence of hallucinations and/or delusions is always abnormal. ________

false

Everyone who assesses a person with mental retardation and apparent psychotic symptoms should consider *stress* as the most likely explanation for such behavior. Additional information may be obtained from check of changes in mood and sleep. Many experts feel that, in a confusing picture with complex presentation, psychosis should be intentionally underdiagnosed. Psychotic disorder is (more or much less?) common than mood disorders in people with mental retardation. ____________________

much less

THE END

REFERENCES

American Psychiatric Association (1994). *Diagnostic and statistical manual of mental disorders* (4th edition). Washington, DC: Author.

Hurley, A. D. (1996). The misdiagnosis of hallucinations and delusions in persons with mental retardation: A neurodevelopmental perspective. *Seminars in Clinical Neuropsychiatry, 1,* 122-133.

GENERAL PRINCIPLES OF PSYCHOTIC DISORDERS IN PERSONS WITH MENTAL RETARDATION

Pretest/Posttest

T F 1. The term "psychosis" includes only conditions which include delusions and/or prominent hallucinations.

T F 2. Delusions are experienced as hearing, seeing, smelling, tasting, or touching something that is not there.

T F 3. When someone is hearing a voice that is not there, he or she may be having an hallucination.

T F 4. A person who hears voices when falling asleep is said to be having an hallucination.

T F 5. A person with disorganized behavior due to a psychosis may be unable to keep himself/herself clean.

T F 6. Degrees of thought disorganization are usually measured by degrees of speech disorganization.

T F 7. Catatonic behavior is diagnostic of psychosis.

T F 8. Hallucinations are considered negative symptoms of schizophrenia.

T F 9. Distinction between true negative symptoms and medication side effects is made by careful clinical assessment.

T F 10. Negative symptoms are very specific, and clearly are different from "normal" behavior.

T F 11. People with negative symptoms of schizophrenia appear sad and uncomfortable.

T F 12. Residual symptoms of schizophrenia often persist for some time after completion of an active phase of the disease.

T F 13. Diagnosis of psychosis cannot be made in persons with mental retardation.

T F 14. Persons with mental retardation have difficulty describing hallucinations and other psychotic symptoms.

T F 15. Diagnostic overshadowing refers to the process of attributing every abnormal behavior to mental retardation rather than a mental health disorder.

T F 16. Diagnostic distortion refers to the process of attributing every abnormal behavior to mental retardation rather than a mental health disorder.

T F 17. Depression is frequently missed when persons with mental retardation are diagnosed as having a psychosis.

T F 18. Persons with mental retardation who experience frequent failures may develop self-gratifying fantasies, which may be mistaken for delusions.

T F 19. Psychosis is often underdiagnosed in persons with mental retardation.

T F 20. The presence of hallucinations and/or delusions is always abnormal.

Name: ______________________________

Position: ____________________________

Date: __________________

GENERAL PRINCIPLES OF PSYCHOTIC DISORDERS IN PERSONS WITH MENTAL RETARDATION

Pretest/Posttest

Answers:

1. True
2. False
3. True
4. False
5. True
6. True
7. False
8. False
9. True
10. False
11. False
12. True
13. False
14. True
15. True
16. False
17. True
18. True
19. False
20. False

PERSONALITY DISORDERS IN PERSONS WITH MENTAL RETARDATION

Instructions for use of this self-directed instruction program:

- Cover the right-hand side of each page, since this gives the answer to the questions.
- Read each section carefully, and WRITE your answer in the designated place.
- After WRITING your answer, check and see if you are correct.
- Refer to your handout materials as necessary.

PERSONALITY DISORDERS IN PERSONS WITH MENTAL RETARDATION

A personality disorder is an enduring pattern of inner experience and behavior that is markedly different from the affected individual's culture. Every person is different from every other person. When differences cause distress or impairment in social, occupational, or other important areas of functioning, then a PERSONALITY DISORDER is said to be present. Personality disorders are (transient or enduring?). ________________

enduring

A person who seems peculiar, but who functions relatively well at work, at home, and in the community, probably (does or doesn't?) have a personality disorder.

____

doesn't (He/she may have a peculiar personality type, but if function is satisfactory, no personality disorder is present.)

People from different cultural backgrounds are apt to act in different ways. Peculiar or unusual behavior that is part of the affected individual's culture (is or is not?) a symptom of a personality disorder.

____

is not

Pattern of a personality disorder is manifested in at least two of the following areas: cognition (way of thinking), affectivity (moodiness), interpersonal functioning, and/or impulse control. Cognition means ways of perceiving and interpreting self, other people, and events. Affectivity means the range, intensity, lability (up-and-down-ness), and appropriateness of emotional response. Ways of perceiving and interpreting self, others, and events make up a process called c________________.

cognition

Enduring patterns of personality disorders are inflexible and pervasive across a broad range of personal and social situations. Patterns symptomatic of a personality disorder are seen in (only a few or a wide variety?) of life situations. ____________________________

a wide variety

Patterns associated with personality disorders are stable and of long duration, with onset often as far back as adolescence or early adulthood. If "state" disorders are relatively short, with a beginning and usually some sort of ending, and "trait" disorders are more pervasive and of long duration, personality disorders can be said to be (state or trait?) disorders. ______________

trait

The term a________________ means the range, intensity, lability, and appropriateness of emotional response.

affectivity

The pattern of a personality disorder is manifested in at least two of the following areas: cognition, affectivity, interpersonal functioning, and/or i_______________ control.

impulse

The ten classified personality disorders in *Diagnostic and Statistical Manual of Mental Disorders* (4th edition) (DSM-IV) are often grouped into three clusters as: odd or eccentric (Paranoid, Schizoid, & Schizotypal), dramatic, emotional, or erratic (Antisocial, Borderline, Histrionic, & Narcissistic), and anxious or fearful (Avoidant, Dependent, & Obsessive-compulsive). The ten DSM-IV classified personality disorders are often grouped into _______ clusters.

3 (Odd or eccentric; Dramatic, emotional, or erratic; and Anxious or fearful)

Persons who appear odd or eccentric, and whose behavior patterns have been present for a long period of time and interfere with life functioning, may have Paranoid, Schizoid, or S_________________ personality disorder.

Schizotypal

An Individual with a long-term history of dramatic, emotional, and/or erratic behavior may have a personality disorder. Among personality disorders to be considered in this instance are Narcissistic, Histrionic, Antisocial, and B________________.

Borderline (This is a very common personality disorder which may interfere greatly with affected individual's life.)

Borderline personality disorder is (rare or common?), and often occurs in the presence of other personality disorders. ___________

common

Individuals with Avoidant, Dependent, and/or Obsessive-compulsive personality disorder usually appear anxious or f______________.

fearful

Many persons may be diagnosed with more than one personality disorder. The presence of more than one personality disorder at the same time is (rare or common?). _______________

common

People with SCHIZOID PERSONALITY DISORDER often seem odd or eccentric. They seem to be detached from social relationships, and have a restricted range of expression of emotions in interpersonal settings. These symptoms begin by early adulthood and are present in a variety of settings. Persons with Schizoid personality disorder appear to show (a lot of or very little?) expression of emotions. ____________

very little

For a diagnosis of Schizoid personality disorder to be made, the affected individual must show at least 4 of 7 listed symptoms. Symptoms include lack of desire for or enjoyment of close relationships (including family), choice of solitary activities, little interest in sexual experiences, lack of pleasure in most activities, and lack of close friends or confidants. Persons with Schizoid personality disorder have (few or many?) friends. ____________

few

Other symptoms of Schizoid personality disorder include apparent indifference to the praise or criticism of others, and emotional coldness, detachment, or "flattened" affectivity. Persons with Schizoid personality disorder (desire or do not want?) close relationships or friendships. ____________

do not want

True or false?: Persons with Schizoid personality disorder appear "happy-go-lucky" and often seek out group activities. ____________

false

Individuals with SCHIZOTYPAL PERSONALITY DISORDER share with Schizoid personality disorder reduced ability to make close relationships. They are very uncomfortable with close relationships, and often have odd beliefs or magical thinking which influences their behavior. These beliefs are not consistent with their cultural norms. People with Schizotypal personality disorder (often or usually don't?) appear strange, eccentric, or peculiar. ____________________

often

People with Schizotypal personality disorder frequently are extremely suspicious of others, and appear emotionally "flat." They often lack close friends, and have a lot of anxiety in social situations. This anxiety tends to be associated with paranoid fears rather than negative judgement about their own capabilities. People who appear eccentric, tend to stay away from others, and believe in magic may have a S____________________ personality disorder.

Schizotypal

An individual who functions relatively well in his/her daily life, but has a strong belief in clairvoyance, telepathy, or "sixth sense" (may or probably doesn't?) have a Schizotypal personality disorder. ____________________

probably doesn't (He/she may have a Schizotypal personality type, but not a disorder, because of good functioning.)

Schizotypal personality disorder is a (state or trait?) condition. ______________

trait

To be diagnosed as having ANTISOCIAL PERSONALITY DISORDER, an individual must be at least 18 years old, and must have shown a pervasive pattern of disregard for and violation of the rights of others, with symptoms occurring since before the age of 15. A person who gets into the "drug culture" at 19 after a rather uneventful earlier life (can or probably shouldn't?) be diagnosed as having Antisocial personality disorder. ____________________

probably shouldn't (since persistent symptoms should have been present before the age of 15)

An individual with Antisocial personality disorder fails to conform to norms of society with respect to lawful behaviors, as indicated by repeatedly performing acts that are grounds for arrest. People with Antisocial personality disorder (often, only occasionally, or almost never?) are well-known to law enforcement officials. ______________________

often (These people are repeat offenders.)

Impulsivity, failure to plan ahead, irritability, aggressiveness, and reckless disregard for the safety of self or others may all be symptoms of Antisocial personality disorder. Persons with Antisocial personality disorder (frequently or usually don't?) get into physical fights or commit physical assaults. ______________

frequently

Consistent irresponsibility associated with Antisocial personality disorder usually is manifested by failure to sustain consistent work behavior or honor financial obligations. Individuals with this disorder show a lack of remorse, and appear indifferent to hurting, mistreating, or stealing from others. People with Antisocial personality disorder appear to have (a very strong or very little?) conscience. ______________________

very little (They often show virtually no true remorse for their actions.)

An individual who repeatedly lies, uses aliases, and "cons" others for personal profit or pleasure, then pretends to be sorry for his/her deeds and promises to reform (but doesn't) may have a(n) ________________ personality disorder.

Antisocial

A man who has mild mental retardation and is arrested because of storing stolen merchandise for family members in his agency-supported apartment (may or probably doesn't?) have Antisocial personality disorder. ____________

probably doesn't (He serves a useful, if illegal and unfortunate, function in his cultural environment—he is important to his family!)

The essential feature of BORDERLINE PERSONALITY DISORDER is a pervasive pattern of instability of self-image, interpersonal relationships, and mood. Persons with Borderline personality disorder generally have (steady or unstable?) moods. ____________

unstable (beginning by early adulthood and present in a variety of life contexts)

Borderline personality disorder is often accompanied by may features of other personality disorders. Persons with Borderline personality disorder (seldom or often?) present with features characteristic of other personality disorders. ____________

often

Persons with Borderline personality disorder often appear "contrary" in social situations and have a generally pessimistic outlook on life. They seem to alternate between desires for dependency and self-assertion. During periods of extreme stress they may have temporary symptoms of psychosis, but these are not usually severe enough to treat with medication. Borderline personality disorder is (rare or common?) in the general population. ____________

common (apparently)

True or false?: People with Borderline personality disorder often appear cheerful and cooperative. ____________

false (!!!)

Persons with Borderline personality disorder (BPD) often make frantic efforts to avoid real or imagined abandonment. Their interpersonal relationships are frequently marked by alternations between idealization and devaluation—they seem to either hate or love people, with these emotions changing frequently, even toward the same person. Persons with Borderline personality disorder have both intense and (stable or unstable?) relationships with significant others. ________________

unstable

People with Borderline personality disorder have a markedly and persistently unstable self-image or sense of self. Persons with BPD (seldom or frequently?) have an identity disturbance. __________________

frequently (Their self-image and/or sense of self may be very disturbed.)

Persons with Borderline personality disorder frequently are impulsive in their behavior. To count as a diagnostic factor this must involve at least two areas that are potentially self-damaging, such as sex, spending, substance abuse, reckless driving, and binge eating. An individual with impulsive behavior that is trivial and usually just involves rash talking (has or does not have?) one criterion for a diagnosis of Borderline personality disorder. ____________________

does not have (at least not a criterion related to impulsive behavior, since rash talking usually is not self-damaging)

People with BPD may exhibit recurrent suicidal behavior, gestures, and/or threats, or may exhibit self-mutilating behavior. A person who picks continuously at his skin until he makes it bleed is exhibiting an example of self-mutilating behavior. Self-injurious behavior (SIB) in persons with mental retardation often is of multi-factorial origin. SIB (never, always, or sometimes?) is a symptom of Bor-

sometimes (People with MR certainly can have BPD, but

derline personality disorder.

____

diagnosis must involve more than just SIB.)

Persons with Borderline personality disorder characteristically are (pessimistic or optimistic?) ____________________

pessimistic

Individuals with Borderline personality disorder often have mood instability, with frequent "ups and downs." Episodes of unhappiness, irritability, or anxiety usually last a few hours, and rarely ever more than a few days. These episodes may, however, occur very frequently. Persons with Borderline personality disorder (may or usually don't?) have periods of sadness that last for months without remission. ____________________

usually don't

In persons with mental retardation the impulsivity associated with Borderline personality disorder may be misdiagnosed as merely "typical MR behavior." Symptoms of unstable and intense interpersonal relationships may lead to poor relationships with staff, peers, and family, as well as over-idealization of some staff members. Borderline personality disorder is (easy to diagnose or frequently overlooked?) in persons with mental retardation.

____

frequently overlooked (While there is no "magic pill" for BPD, knowledge of diagnosis does facilitate assessment and treatment planning.)

Individuals with BPD frequently have chronic feelings of emptiness and often complain of an inability to truly enjoy their experiences. This may show up in a person with mental retardation as nonspecific complaints about life and current programming. A man with mild mental retardation who looks forward to going to work and likes the people there (may or probably doesn't?) have Borderline personality disorder.

____

probably doesn't

A woman with severe mental retardation who complains about getting up and getting to her sheltered workshop assignment, but who functions well when she gets there and interacts freely with peers while there, probably (does or does not?) have Borderline personality disorder. ______________________

does not (Someone who is functioning well shouldn't be diagnosed as having any kind of personality disorder.)

Borderline personality disorder is often considered difficult to treat. Staff at St. John's Mercy Medical Center in St. Louis use a communication system, "SET," for persons with BPD in crisis: "S" = t (a personal statement of concern); "E" = Empathy (acknowledging the person's chaotic feelings); and "T" = Truth (Reality) (the individual's responsibility for his/her own life." Therapists for someone with BPD (should or shouldn't?) take responsibility for his/her life. ______________

shouldn't (Attempts to help by others cannot pre-empt this primary responsibility.)

On occasion a general medical condition may result in a persistent personality disturbance that represents a change from the individual's previous behavior pattern. If that change results in significant distress or impairment in important areas of functioning, the person is said to have PERSONALITY CHANGE DUE TO GENERAL MEDICAL CONDITION, formerly called Organic personality disorder. Medical conditions (may or usually don't?) lead to personality changes. ________________

may

Personality change due to general medical condition may be of various types, as labile, disinhibited, aggressive, apathetic, paranoid, or others. An individual who becomes persistently irritable and aggressive after a head injury may have Personality change due to __________ __________ __________.

General medical condition (formerly Organic personality disorder)

One type of Personality change due to general medical condition is called "COCKTAIL PARTY SYNDROME," characteristically associated with hydrocephalus. Persons with this condition have speech that is chatty, with superficial content. There is little content in relation to verbal fluency, and speech is characterized by short, stereotyped phrases. Persons with a history of hydrocephalus who are quite "chatty" may have c__________ __________ __________.

cocktail party syndrome (This is a neuropsychologic condition.)

In addition to chatty speech, persons with cocktail party syndrome often have poor judgement, and are emotionally labile. Their I.Q. is often in a range of mental retardation, and there is a significant difference between verbal and performance I.Q.. They also frequently have visual-perceptual deficits. In persons with cocktail party syndrome, __________ I.Q. is higher than performance I.Q..

verbal

The general medical condition associated with cocktail party syndrome is h__________.

hydrocephalus

Often staff and family members of persons with cocktail party syndrome fail to have a realistic sense of that individual's abilities, and expect far more than the person can produce in terms of vocational and academic goals. Pressure from others may cause the person to blame himself/herself for failing to live up to the expectations, and may result in anxiety and depression. Persons with cocktail party syndrome (usually do or often don't?) live up to the expectations of others. ____________________

often don't (if those expectations are unrealistic)

Another disorder involving personality development is DISSOCIATIVE IDENTITY DISORDER, formerly called Multiple personality disorder. In this condition two or more distinct identities or personality states exist, each with its own relatively enduring pattern of relating to the environment and self. This is a rare condition, but can occur in people with mental retardation as well as in the general population. Dissociative identity disorder is (rare or common?). ______________

rare

In Dissociative identity disorder at least two of the identities or personality states recurrently take control of the person's behavior. This condition (can or never?) occur(s) in persons with developmental disabilities. ______________

can (This is, however, extremely rare.)

While personality disorders are not in general felt to be responsive to drug treatment, knowledge about these diagnoses can be of great help to members of interdisciplinary teams and others who are attempting to plan effective programs for persons with developmental disabilities, since other treatment modalities such as environmental changes and group therapy may be helpful. Knowledge of any psychiatric diagnosis (may help or is irrelevant to?) program planning. ________________

may help (This is probably the understatement of the year!)

THE END

PERSONALITY DISORDERS IN PERSONS WITH MENTAL RETARDATION

Educational Objectives

Participants will be able to answer the following questions:

1. What are the characteristics of personality disorders in general?

2. What are specific diagnostic criteria for personality disorders that may be relatively commonly seen in persons with mental retardation and other developmental disabilities?

3. How does knowledge of the presence of a personality disorder facilitate the planning process for persons with developmental disabilities?

PERSONALITY DISORDERS IN PERSONS WITH MENTAL RETARDATION

Pretest/Posttest

T F 1. Personality disorders are considered "state" conditions rather than "trait" conditions.

T F 2. Peculiar-appearing people who function relatively well at work, at home, and in the community probably do not have a personality disorder.

T F 3. Patterns of behavior in personality disorders are enduring, inflexible, and pervasive across a broad range of personal and social situations.

T F 4. Borderline personality disorder is very rare in the general population, and even rarer in people with mental retardation.

T F 5. People with Avoidant, Dependent, and/or Obsessive Compulsive personality disorder(s) usually appear anxious or fearful.

T F 6. The presence of more than one personality disorder at the same time is rare.

T F 7. Persons with Schizoid personality disorder are often happy, and often seek out group activities.

T F 8. Persons with Schizoid personality disorder show very little emotional expression.

T F 9. A person who functions relatively well in his/her daily life, but has a strong belief in extraterrestrial beings probably does not have Schizotypal personality disorder.

T F 10. Schizotypal personality disorder is a trait condition.

T F 11. People with Antisocial personality disorder are often well-known to law enforcement officials.

T F 12. People with Antisocial personality disorder appear to have a very strong conscience.

T F 13. People with Borderline personality disorder generally have very unstable moods.

T F 14. Persons with Borderline personality disorder often present with features characteristic of other personality disorders.

T F 15. People with Borderline personality disorder often appear cheerful and cooperative.

T F 16. Self-injurious behavior is always a symptom of Borderline personality disorder.

T F 17. In persons with mental retardation the impulsivity associated with Borderline personality disorder may be misdiagnosed as merely "typical MR behavior."

T F 18. Effective therapists for persons with Borderline personality disorder usually take over responsibilities for the individual's life decisions.

T F 19. Persons with "cocktail party syndrome: have a past history of hydrocephalus.

T F 20. Previous name for Dissociative identity disorder is Organic personality disorder

Name: ______________________ Date: ____________

PERSONALITY DISORDERS IN PERSONS WITH MENTAL RETARDATION

Pretest/Posttest

Answers

1. False
2. True
3. True
4. False
5. True
6. False
7. False
8. True
9. True
10. True
11. True
12. False
13. True
14. True
15. False
16. False
17. True
18. False
19. True
20. False

REFERENCES

American Psychiatric Association (1994). *Diagnostic and Statistical Manual of Mental Disorders* (4th ed.). Washington, DC: Author.

Hurley, A. D. & Sovner, R. (1988). The clinical characteristics and management of Borderline Personality Disorder in mentally retarded persons, Psychiatric Aspects of Mental Retardation Reviews, 7 (#7 & #8).

Hurley, A. D. & Sovner, R. (1995). Six cases of patients with mental retardation who have Antisocial Personality Disorder, *Psychiatric Services, 46*, 828-831.

Kreisman, J. J. & Straus, H. (1989). *I hate you—don't leave me: Understanding the borderline personality.* New York: Avon Books.

Links, P. S. (1990. *Family environment and Borderline Personality Disorder*. Washington, DC: American Psychiatric Press.

Livesley, W. J. (Ed.) (1995). *The DSM-IV personality disorders.* New York: Guilford Press.

Oates, W. E. (1987). *Beyond the masks: Personality disorders in religious behavior*. Louisville, KY: Westminster Press.

Skodol, A. E. (1989). *Problems in differential diagnosis: From DSM-III to DSM-III-R in clinical practice.* Washington, DC: American Psychiatric Press.

Widiger, T. A. & Frances, A. J. (1988). Personality disorders, in J. A. Talbott, R. E. Hales, & S. C. Yudofsky (Eds.*), Textbook of Psychiatry*. Washington, DC: American Psychiatric Press.

Widiger, T. A. & Gunderson, J. G. (Section Eds.) (1992). Severe personality disorders, In A. Tasman & M. B. Riba (Eds.), *Review of Psychiatry, Volume 11*. Washington, DC: American Psychiatric Press.